OVERTHINKING

How to Declutter Your Mind, Remove Anxiety and Daily Stress, and Improve Your Social and Working Life

JOSEPH RUIZ

TABLE OF CONTENTS

INTRODUCTION

For some years now, the human race has become more engrossed in unlocking its inner creativity to build a more conducive environment for itself, which is a product of the mind. The mind is not just the seat of creativity, but also of confusion, happiness, sadness, peace and joy; it all depends on what you make of it.

Ever since Descartes made his intellectual assertion that "I think, therefore I am" *Cogito, ergo sum"* the battle betweenevil andgood, right and wrong, slavery and freedom has shifted to the mind; hence you need to have a full grip of your thoughts by avoiding overthinking, anxiety disorder, and fear so that you can become the kind of individual that will be useful and happy in the world that we live in.I want to employ you to challenge the notion that we function best and get the maximum enjoyment that life has to offer when we're continuously engrossed in non-stop worrying and thinking. We need to embrace the concept that "a peaceful mind is the most productive mind".

Theeffect of multiple psychological pollutants in modernday society cannot be overemphasised, so the goal of writing this book is to help you get a full grasp of what it takes to have control over your mind and reinvent the new you.

You will learn

> ➢ The nine negative effects of overthinking

- ➤ Ten strategies to conqueroverthinking

- ➤ How to take full control of your mind

- ➤ Everything you need to know about anxiety and how to eliminate it for good

- ➤ Everything you need to know about stress and how it affects your productivity, cognitive thinking and your health

- ➤ Develop and harness the power of positive emotions

- ➤ How to use cognitive therapy to permanently eliminate anxiety and stress

- ➤ How to permanently build your self-esteem

- ➤ How to develop the ultimate best version of you.

CHAPTER 1

What is Overthinking?

Overthinking is a loop of unproductive thoughts. It can also be described as spending an excess amount of time thinking about an issue. Overthinking is when you overanalyze every situation or the steps you want to take to do something.

Some mental health illnesses where a person can't stop their brain from overthinking are trauma, panic disorder, social anxiety disorder, phobias, PTSD, agoraphobia, or a symptom of some other diseases.

Overthinking is the types of thought that everyone has struggled from at some point in their life. Overthinking, for some may havestarted in grade school when you were asked to write a short essay, and you spent more time thinking abouthow to make your work look perfect even though it already was, rather than actually writing it.

It could be those minuteswhen you ponder about the label on the pack of a cookie, and you wonder if it is suitable for you. Overthinking is more common in the workplace when you think over an issue instead of taking actions and doings things that will fix the problem.It is quite a common misconception to confuse overthinking with deep thinking.The fundamental difference is overthinking occurs when you ponder over a situation in a way that doesn't make the situation any better while deep thinking is more of a constructive thought that puts all points of view into consideration.

Overthinkers arepeople who;

- Have a false impression that they're gaining insights by overthinking about a particular problem.

- Have histories of abuse, which could be sexual,violence or bullying.

- Have a personality trait that demands perfection.

- See their daily activities as an uncontrollable stressor.

The effects of Overthinking

<u>Stress</u>

Chronic overthinkers spend a considerable amount of their time playing over past interactions, past events, and conversations in their head. They focus on regretting their past choices, daydreaming about the future as well as giving in to their fearsduring their thought process.Theyregularly ponder about what things mean and why they happened.Stress occurs when you overthink past setbacks, or relationship breakups and every sorrowful thing that happens around you. It is not those things in itself that causes stress, it is when you overthink about the supposed problem, that is what leads to stress.

It can affect your health. Overthinking is a result of excessive activity in the left hemisphere of your brainwhich can leave you with significant disruptions in both your physical and mental state. Overthinking places you more in your head than in reality, you can live in your head so much that you then become addicted tothis state, and when you're in your head for so long, it leads to somatic complaints such as a headache. Difficulty in making decisions as a result of overthinking, you find it challenging to make decisions and stick to them.You will therefore find yourself constantly switching between resolutions and never actually sticking to them.When you're presented with a choice, the usual way to select what you want is to think about the options before you then decide on which option you'll prefer. When you are overthinking you continue pondering over the option that you prefer and the ones you'll be doing away with, this continued zig-zag thought won't make youdecide on time, and when you finally do, you'll have problems forgetting about the alternative option.Overthinking affects your ability to make decisions and focus totally on them to successfully carry them out.

You Miss Opportunities

Your thoughts start to imprison you and you will find yourself continually missing opportunities. Your thought patternsput you in a rut which makes you unableto seeyour usual viewpoint, feelings and beliefs. This negativethought processwon't allow you to embrace different thoughts as you will begin to overanalyse them, you will enlarge the disadvantage of going outside your viewpoint more than necessary,locking up your mind in a prison youyourself have created. When you dispose of this habit, you will be able to allow different thoughts to enter your environment. Overthinking will prevent you from viewing things from a much more diverse perspective.

It Can Drive Away Social Support.

Overthinking impairs your reasoning capabilities, and as a result, it can drive your critical social support away. Your social supportarethose friends and family members that you turn to when you requireadvice, help or even financial assistance.They arethe first people you turn to when you need help solving a problem.You're probably wondering how and why your overthinking habit will drive away these individuals that love you and can't do without you, here's how your overthinking will drive a wedge between you and them;

Overthinkers magnify problems beyond what they are, so you mayfind yourself continually reaching out to your family and friends for support. This constant reaching out can seem pleasant to them at first, but as time goes on, it will begin to constitute a nuisance. The constant bickering might quickly wear them out if they are approached too many times than they desire, especially if it is about the same old worry. When you fail to get over your problem, your social support begins to act dismissive,and they may gradually start avoiding you. This loss can lead to a feeling of conflict and social rejection, which further drives you down the long road of overthinking.

You Become Passive.

Overthinking saps your sense of control and will make you a passive person instead of being an active person who takes action and makes things happen. Overthinking doesn't let people make up their mind about putting their foot down to accomplish a meaningful goal. You allow every bit of information that enters your mind to be a piece of information to why you should not make those essential moves. Meeting every target requires thinking, planning, and action, however, overthinking makes you think, fret and analyse them without taking corresponding steps. Overthinking weakens your ability to focus.

When your mind is free, calm and not stuck in a loop of unproductive thoughts, it is easier to focus your mind on your goals, studies, work and any other project you have. Overthinking won't give you full control of your mind, and as a result, your mind is always occupied with nonstop thinking over factors you have no control over.

Overthinking makes life boring.

When you allocate so much time to think about things that don't matter, and then rethink about that same matter again, it makes you miss out on life. You spend more time thinking about things than actually doing them.

It Causes Insomnia.

When you're overthinking about what happened in the day because the day is filled with so many activities or you remembered some memorable events in the day, it can cause sleeplessness. To an extent, everyone thinks about what happened in the day, but an overthinker tends to focus on this activity, as such, the body becomes used to the overthinking at night thus it programs itself to be awake at night.

Positive and Healthy Steps to overcome overthinking

Take Action Immediately (If you can)

Overthinkers are stuck in the analysis phase of a problem; they never really take steps based on what they've analysed. If what you're overthinking about is specific, try to focus your mind on the solutions to that problem, then write the answer on a sticky note. Focus your mind on the positive action that you're expecting. For example, instead of"I'm stuck in debt", write,"I need to start earning enough to pay off my debts". Then make plans to expand your network and skills that will make you receive more. You might not get to do anything if your focus is on whether you offended John when you turned down that offer, or whether or not going to that baseball game with your friends will make them detest you. If you can't let go of the worry, call John and tell him why you had to decline. The majority of the timeoverthinkers are engrossed in worrying about how people feel when those that you worry about are actually enjoying themselves.

<u>Challenge YourBeliefs Through Cognitive Restructuring</u>

Overthinkers the majority of the time suffer from "Cognitive distortions". Cognitive distortions are exaggerated and irrational thoughts; it is our minds convincing us that something that is not true is right.

The overthinker's inner voice can tell themthat "your boss didn't speak to you today because he was disappointed in your work", while the truth may be that he was having a bad day; this type of response is one that exaggerates a perceived shortcoming. Your overthinking mind has just played a trick on your worry. Instead of dwelling onthe problem, try to cultivate a little psychological distance by generating other positive interpretationsof the problem that make you doubt your cognitive distortion. This is called "cognitive restructuring".

<u>UnderstandingCognitive Restructuring</u>

Cognition restructuring is a prevalent technique used in tackling overthinking. Cognitive restructuring is designed based on the principle of cognitive meditation, which states that "what we feel does not invariably reflect what happens to us". the technique works on how we respond to what happens to us. The cognitive restructuring technique will help you to organise how you react to a seemingly bad occurrence and make sense of the difficult experience.

Why it works-:

- It assists us to be mentally organized; just like writing a to-do list makes us feel in control when working on a big project, cognitive restructuring will help you to get your mental space more organised.

- It helps us to slow down; if you can slow your thoughts down, then you're almost there on conquering overthinking. Negative thoughts lead to negative emotion; when you notice that those thoughts are coming back, you can shut them down with cognitive restructuring.

- It helps us think more rationally; By encouraging us to question and examine the thoughts that come out of our head, and our first line of thinking, we'll overcome overthinking in no time. When we question our thought patterns and viewpoints, we'll see errors or mistakes in what and how we think. Being able to identify distortions is vitalin solving this problem.

How ToDo Cognitive Restructuring -:

Having understood what cognitive restructuring is, let's delveinto how to engage in cognitive restructuring.

- **Hit the Pause Button**

This method can be beneficial in multiple situations. However, the best time to use cognitive restructuring is when you notice that you're beginning to spend more time than you should, pondering over an issue. When you find yourself in this situation, take a pause and tell yourself that "I shouldn't be doing this".

- __Identify TheTrigger__

Once you've paused your thought, the next thing is to identify the event that made you start overthinking. The event that triggers overthinking is always something that happens in our environment whether it is something that we could have done better, or thatoccurred somewhere and we're wondering about what will happen if a similar event happens to us. An example of such a trigger is when you hear about a massive downsizing in a company, thoughts about an impending recession etc. To help you identify the trigger, ask yourself the question what, who, when and where. Who was present when the thought started? what happened before you started the session of overthinking? when did I start overthinking? and where did it all occur?

- __Notice Your Automatic Thoughts__

Automatic thoughts are our initial interpretation of the event in our head. These thoughts are usually spontaneous, and they typically come in the form of memories, images or verbal self-talk. For example, if you received an email from your boss late at night, your automatic thought could be "Oh no! What's wrong?" I must have forgotten to send him that report. Everyone has automatic thoughts, but a lot of us don't take note of them as they are always instantaneous. When trying to solve overthinking, taking note of those instant thoughts and acting on them might help.

- **<u>Identify and note how intense your emotional reactions are</u>**

Emotions are a product of our mental interpretation of an event that occurred, and the feelingthat it produces is a reflection of our thoughts. If you've been overthinking, you'll find yourself having a lot of negative emotions.

- **<u>Have AnAlternative Thought.</u>**

Once you've identified the trigger, take note of your automatic thought when it occurs, and take note of your reaction, you should come up with alternative thoughts when overthinking is trying to slip into your mind. For example, if someone overtakes you recklessly, and it almost leads to a collision, instead of cursing at the driver and thinking of how a friend or a celebrity died that way, you can simply say to yourself "Wow that was scary, we've got bad drivers everywhere, so I'm not surprised", then focus on your journey. If you are currently experiencing an unfortunate situation, you can generate two or three alternative thoughts. For example, if you were diagnosed with cancer, instead of overthinking the situation, when you notice the thought, let your alternative thought to be "I do not have control over my circumstances, I will enjoy every day".

- **<u>Re-rate Your Response.</u>**

Take note of the effect of saying these alternatives to yourself; you should notice a considerable improvement and ensure that you stick to this habit.

Redirect Your Attention

Find an engaging activity that you love. This engaging activity can be; taking a brisk walk with a friend,playingfootballat the stadium, you can also challenge someone to play the game of chess with you etc.The activity should be one that combines social contact and mental engagement. Some activities that you can easily engage in include calling up someone you're emotionally attached to, playing with your pet or children. When you're stuck in traffic, you can listen to a recorded standup comedy, an audiobook or stimulating radio talk.

- ### **Consciously Overthink Things**

This technique works by breaking up old mentalpatterns and replacing those patterns with new and positive ones. In this technique, simplify things and try to see the humour in overthinking everything. Realise that it is when we're calm and peaceful on the inside that we can reach our full potential. Assuming you're preparing for a presentation and you're overthinking everything that could go wrong in the presentation. Take some moment to extremely overthink the scenario,butdo this in a funny way. Ask yourself questions like, what are the exciting examples you can give? What are all the different ways you could arrange your slide? What are the things that you can do right now to keep yourself focused on the presentation? What are the different objections that the listeners might have? Find the humour in going extreme with this, imagine that you can duplicate yourself into multiple places and address everyone in the audience. Imagine that you have five arms and you're trying to type so fast to cover all bases, you're typing so fast that the heat from your head is making the fire alarm sound. With a renewed sense of focus, imagine yourself trying to make an excellent presentation with what you currently have on your slide.

- <u>Get Some Exercise</u>

The only thing that can be compared to when anindividual exercises is pushing the reboot button on your computer. Anytime you take time to exercise; you will always come back to your house in a better state of mind. Your overthinking tendency goes above the roof if you have tons of energy that you haven't burnt off. Exercising relieves mental tension. It is like tapping the refresh button on a page.

- <u>Breathe Calmly (Pranayama)</u>

The way you breathe is a direct representation of your state of mind. Do you doubt this? Take ten deep breaths when you are worrying about something, then take the same deep breath when you feel a bit relaxed; you will notice a difference between the ways you breathe, guaranteed. Pranayama has been a longstanding practice in yoga, and it is seen as a prerequisite for those with plans to reach a higher level of consciousness. It gives the same result as going for a walk or any other physical exercise.

- ### Gaze Fixing

Yoga experts will tell you that your eyes tell a lot of stories about your mental state; well, I also had doubts until I did some research. It is a widely proven fact that the erratic movement of your eyes indicates overactivity in your mind.

When you find yourself overthinking, calm yourself down and fix your eyes on one spot for a few minutes. Blink regularly and make sure you have a calm and relaxed gaze. Your mind becomes calmer as you calm your eyes.

- ### Take a Nap

Don't follow those who believe that taking a nap is a sign of laziness; such individuals are a ticking timebomb of diseases. Naps are really underrated. A thirty-minute rest will make you feel very relaxed; you will think better. It is often said of Albert Einstein that he had his breakthrough inventions anytime he took a break from his problem.

- ### Change Your Environment

Changing your environment can do a lot in encouraging you to embrace new ways of thinking. When you directly look at the stars in the sky at night, they disappear, but when you look at them from a peripheral vision, they reappear. This is an analogy to what a change of environment can do for you.

If you find yourself stuck in the loop of overthinking, change your location. Go to the library, a coffee shop or a park. Check out neighbourhoods that are different from yours, surround yourself with people with a different mindset from those you've been interacting with, talk about new things. Stop thinkingabout your problems and start working on trying to solve them.

- **<u>Avoid Talking It Out</u>**

It is a great idea to brainstorm solutions with friends and colleagues, but when the topic is something that triggers overthinking for you, avoid it. When you dissect and revisit the negative information of what triggers it with someone that is prone to co-rumination. You might be tempted to believe that it solves the problem, but it doesn't, it only sends you into the deeper corners of overthinking.

- **<u>Be Patient</u>**

Overthinking is not a problem that disappears in an instant; as such, you may struggle for a while. However, you'll gradually master how to control it with more practice. As awkward as this may sound, your mind is tempted to overthink why you have a problem overthinking. Recognise that this is a mere extension of the problem. Seek the help of a therapist if persistent overthinking interferes with your life.

How to Take Control of Your Mind.

Your mind is the most potent instrument for the creation of everything you desire, and if not tightly controlled, it can be a mighty destructive force. The mind, as intangible as it is, can breakdown the very thing that houses it, which is the body.

Your mind affects your perception, and you know what they say; perception is the reality.

It is said that an average human thinks around 65,000 thoughts every 24hours, now that's a lot. A lot of times, these thoughts are usually selfabusive, unproductive and a waste of mental energy.

You can let the energy of your mind to flow in what direction youwish, in fact, they would naturally do unless you rechannel them to a more productive thing, it is time to take control of your thoughts.

You need to decide to be an individual who consciously channels the direction of theirthoughts.Be the one controlling your mind; don't let it be your master. When you change your thoughts, you will be able to change the feelings they produce as well. You will also be able to eliminate and identify those things that trigger your unwanted feelings, reducing these feelings help you achieve a state where your mind is at peace. Everyone that has mastered the art of selfmindcontrol achieves more than those who have not.

Who Is Thinking ForMe?

You need to realise that your mind is the abode of many settlers, and they are in control of the thoughts that come out of your mind. To master these settlers, you need to have a full grasp of who they are, and what they feed on so you can take charge and send them packing.

Here are the residents in your mind that breed those unhealthy and unproductive thoughts; they are the real culprit.

The Inner Critic.

They are the abusive words that you've housed over time; they consist of

- The thoughts you've created from the expectation of other people.

- Comparing yourself to others, including celebrities and those you look up to.

- Other people's words, mostly your family members.

- The words you've said to yourself at those moments of rejection and betrayal. Your interpretation of the betrayals and moments of rejections creates self-blame and self-doubt.

Pain, lack of self-love, lack of self-acceptance and low self-esteem are what feeds the inner critic in you.

The Anxious

This mind occupant lives in the future. With this occupant, it is always what if?Theconcern is always about how the future will turn out. The primary motivator for anxiety is fear, and the causeof fear is always something unreasonable. Past occurrences usually trigger anxiety.

The Reactor

This mind occupant is also known as a trouble maker; it triggers pain, anger and frustration. It is also a victim of unhealed wounds from the past. Any experience/scenario that is closely identical to the past event will trigger it. So many things can set off the reactor, some of which include smells, feelings, words and sounds.

The Sleep Depriver

The sleep depriver is a combination of the activities of many mind occupants. The sleep depriver, as the name connotes deprives you of those precious time of the night. The things that trigger the sleep depriver include;

- Working at night to take care of business you've neglected or you were too busy to work on during the day.

- Generalized anxiety, selfdoubt and low self-esteem.

- If your mind hates silence.

- A combination of the worrier and inner critic.

Mastering the Mind

Your thoughtshave to be observed; you must take cognisance of who is running the show, this will help you to know what technique will help you master your mind.

Start each day with the intention of focusing on your thoughts and analysing the ideas they produce, try to catch yourself thinking unwanted thoughts.

You can control your mind with two techniques, they are;

Technique A –Try interrupting and replacing them

Technique B – Eliminate the thoughts

When you use Technique A, it reprograms your subconscious mind, if you keep to this process, the thoughts that you replace them with will become your "go-to" thoughts after a while. Technique B is what is called "Peace of mind". For the inner critic and worrier, use technique A, while technique B works perfectly well for the sleep depriver and reactor.

Let's explain how to counter each thought;

<u>Inner critic;</u>

When you start thinking of those thoughts that fall into this category (berating yourself, calling yourself names and disrespecting yourself), interrupt it immediately. You can tell yourself (in your mind) to stop, say "Enough! I'm in charge now." Then, replace the negative thoughts with a counter thought that begins with "I am." For example, if your thought was, "I am a failure", replace it with "I am going to succeed though I sometimes fail, who doesn't anyway." You can also have a little talk with yourself; the conversation should not enhance the opinion of your inner critic; it should discredit it and make it look insane for saying the things it says.

For example, you can say "Just because John said I'm a failure, thatdoesn't make me one, Albert Einstein could have been called a loser because he failed in so many experiments, but he's still regarded as a success. Speak words that you want to hearyourself, and give the reason why those words are valid.

You can write out your counter thoughts if you notice that you suffer from a recurring self-critical thought. You should not giveup when evicting this squatter. Here are some reasons why you shouldn't accommodate these thoughts henceforth;

- The name you call yourself becomes some trigger when others call you that same name; as such, this thought pattern also maintains the presence of a reactor.

- They become a platform for the worrier to act on.

- They are emotionally and verbally abusive and a bully.

- They destroy the self-esteem of anyone who houses them; they tell you that you're not worthy. If you continue to hear these words every day, you will subconsciously start to believe it.

When you eliminate this thought process, you will diminish the activity of the other three.

<u>The Worrier</u>

Prolonged worrying is emotionally, physically and mentally unhealthy and as such, can lead to longterm health complications. What creates worrying is the fight or flight response created by fear. Once worrying begins to creep in, you should recognise it immediately by how you feel. Some of the symptoms that fear causes are;

- An increase in blood pressure, the rate of your heartbeat, and a surge in adrenaline.

- Muscular tension

Once you notice those symptoms, use any of the methods described above to replace your thought of worry for gratitude. If you believe in God, this is the time to pray to one, thankhim or her for the gift of life and all you think he or she hasdone for you.

If you have a loved one in distress and you want to say a prayer for them, you can do so. When you say the prayer, smile and try to visualise who you're praying for, say your prayer in the present tense, both of this will help you feel better.

Now take a deep, slow breath through your nose, and slowly through your mouth. When you replace fearful thoughts with gratitude, it will decrease reactionary thinking and behaviour.

For example, if you go to the museum with your child, and theyget lost, and you get angry at the child, it introduces fear to the child. It makes the child believe that "Mummy will get angry if I make mistakes". As such, the child will lie and keep things from you in the future. When such an event happens, change those fearful thoughts with more positive things like "I've got a brilliantchild or my child is quite inquisitive."

The Reactor

The feelings of the reactor activate the flight and fight response, just like the worrier. The signs of the presence of this settler are usually the same as the worrier. However, some differences between the characteristics that both attributeshave are that the reactor exhibits pain, anger, anxiety and frustration, while the worrier exhibits none of those.

When you notice those, you can try to counter those feelings by practising *conscious breathing*. Just as the name sounds, *conscious breathing* is breathing consciously, focus your attention on the air going out and coming into your nostrils. Here's how to perform the exercise.

Breathe in through your nose;

- Gently feel the air as it's entering through your nose

- Feel as your lungs fill and expand

- Feel as the muscles in your belly expand

Breathe out through your nose;

- Feel as your lungs are emptying

- Feel as the muscles in your stomach contract

- Feel the air coming out of your nose, pay attention to the soothing effect that it leaves inyour nose.

Do this continuously till you feel that your adrenaline has normalised. One problem that this squatter causes is that it empowers the sleep depriver, it is like a fuel to it. One major area that suffers as a result of this settler is that it strains your relationship with your romantic lover.

The Sleep Depriver

The sleep depriver is most commonly a perfectionist and a very emotionalperson. It usually emanates from not being able to turn off your mind on time, and it can prevent you from getting muchneeded rest and a restorative night's sleep. Here's how to get rid of this problem.

- Start by focusing on your breathing (Read up mindful breathing in the section above)

- Start imagining the word "in" while breathing in, and the word "out" while breathing out. Elongate the pronunciation to match the length of what you proclaim. For more difficult nights, increase your attention by looking upwards.

Another technique that you can use isto;

- If you wake up too soon, fall back to sleep

- Shutdown your thinking with any of the methods described above

- Calm your feelings

- Keep your mind on the present.

Your mind is a potent tool, and whether you use this tool for a constructive or destructive purpose depends on how much control you have over it.

Your mind can be your biggest supporter, best friend or your oppressor. The choice is yours!

CHAPTER 2

2.1. What is Anxiety?

Anxiety is your body's response to the feeling of fear or uncertainty about what is to come. Some of the symptoms synonymous with fear include:

- Rapid breathing

- Racing heart

- A "burst" of energy

- Butterflies in your stomach

Everyone feels anxious at times; whether it's your first day in school, giving a speech or going for a job interview, this feeling is quite a regular thing. Anxiety can be a way for our body to keep us safe from harm. For example, imagine you're taking a walk through the forest, and you're dragging your feet because you're tired; however, you seesomething that looks like a bear or a snake at the corner of your eyes. You will suddenly forget that you're tired and feel a burst of energy that helps you get away from that location.

If you feel anxious about an assignment that is due, anxiety will motivate you and can help you get it done faster than you earlier thoughts. However, when you start feeling anxious about something unusual, then it can be very unhealthy. Unhealthy anxiety is what is known as an anxiety disorder. Any anxiety that impacts on your daily life is a disorder. Rather than have anxiety as a response to danger, the person with a disorder begins to feel anxious in situations that are perfectly normal like taking a means of public transport or meeting new people.

2.2. CAUSES OF ANXIETY

Explaining what causes anxiety is one of the toughest questions to answer. It's not like flu or malaria. You can't sleep all fine the previous day and wake up with an anxiety disorder because you didn't have a shower the previous day or because you ate something that your body is reacting to. Anxiety disorder is a type of condition that is forged over the years. Every experience you've ever had can determine whether you'll have an anxiety disorder or not. Anxiety disorder has an upbringing component, an environmental component, and a genetic component. If you have an anxiety disorder, it may be as a result of one or a combination of some of these components. Anxiety may even have no apparent cause at all.

Anxiety comes in different forms, and each of those forms hasvarious causes. There are different causes of panic attacks,generalized anxiety, phobias, OCD, PTSD. Every experience of anxiety is unique in some ways. Let us help you understand the cause of the illness better by breaking it into two main causes:

- Biological causes.

- Environmental causes.

Biological Causes of Anxiety Disorders

 The role of genetics and biology in the creation of an anxiety disorder can't be underrated. Anxiety disorders have been known to ruin beautiful relationships, and the thought that people can be born with this unenviable gift is saddening. If you take two people with the same way of life and make a comparison, you willdiscover that one may have an anxiety disorder and the other doesn't. The only difference between the two may be influenced by the body and not the mind. Some noteworthy biological causes of anxiety include.

Deregulation of Brain Chemistry

Many researchers have proven that anxiety can be caused by brain chemical imbalances. These researchers concluded that people with anxiety disorders have issues with some neurotransmitters like norepinephrine, gamma-aminobutyric acid (GABA), and serotonin. It cannot be proven if these imbalances came first or the imbalances are a result of poor coping strategies. Without any serious medical intervention, therapy on its own can improve the chemical regulation in your brain, which indicates that the mind can overcome these biological components and enhance the flow of these chemicals to the brain.

In some cases, doctors prescribe medications that can improve neurotransmitter regulation, and you will undoubtedly see improvements even with small doses. This is an indication that you can alter how theneurotransmitter functions, both environmentally and medically. Some of these neurotransmitters also play a role in emotional stability, sleep and mood, each of which can determine whether you have an anxiety disorder or not.

Brain Activity Alteration

Research has proven through brain imaging that people with an anxiety disorder have different brain activity thanthose without the disorder. Those with an anxiety disorder have been noticed to have anomalies in brain metabolism and blood flow, as well as some structural abnormalities in some parts of their brain. Don't let this scare you if you have anxiety. Studies have proven that with the right treatment, these anomalies can be reversed. In other words, if the reason for the change was an external factor, it can still be improved with the right and effective treatment. These changes are not being caused by anxiety;instead, they are the cause of your anxiety, which invariably means that they will disappear when your anxiety is treated.

Genetics

Studies have revealed that genetics can be a factor in determiningif an individual will developan anxiety disorder. Anxiety disorders, especially panic disorder,can get passed down from parents and immediate family members to their children.

It is not clear what percentage is related to upbringing, because research has shown that children who live with a foster parent with an anxiety disorder tend to get anxious themselves. Those with immediate family members that suffer from an anxiety disorder should work on reducing anxiety and stress in their lives.

Medical Factors

This is quite uncommon, though, but there have always beenreports of medical conditions that led to anxiety. This happens as a result of some illness or disease affecting the normal functioning of the brain, thus disrupting the chemistry of the brain. To treat anxiety in a situation like this, you have to researchthe underlying condition.

Since you were not born with the condition, we can categorise it under environmental factors that cause anxiety. But it is still best referred to as anxiety caused by your biology.

Cases of diseases and illnesses causing anxiety are less common than people imagine, and anxiety can put you in a panic mode that you have this condition even when it has not been medically proven. Some conditions that cause anxiety includes allergies, hypoglycaemia, sleep apnea, asthma, cancer, COPD, celiac disease, high blood pressure, hormonal imbalance, hypertension, hyperthyroidism, lupus, the menopause, mental retardation, mitral valve prolapse, multiple sclerosis, PMS, prostate problems, TMJ and Seizures.

➢ Environmental Causes of Anxiety Disorders.

Anxiety in most people is caused by environmental factors rather than biological factors. However, it is not easy to determine which factor is responsible for an anxiety disorder. In some cases; some are just there and are non-traceable to theroot.

Even if you have cases of anxiety among some of your family members, your environment will still play a vital role in determining if you will developan anxiety disorder or not. It is highly believed that environmental factors act as a trigger to the problem, and it has a significant role in determining if you will developan anxiety disorder or not. In some cases, the environment has been identifiedas the cause of the disorder and not just the trigger.

Environmental factors, when discussing anxiety causes, refers to anything that is not genetic. It refers to the effect of the environment on your mind when we consider every place you have ever been to, everything you've been taught and every experience you have had.

According to a research carried out on dizygotic twins (fraternal twins), and monozygotic twins (identical twins), monozygotic twins who both share the same DNA are twice as like to develop anxiety disorders than fraternal twins. But in all the cases studied, it was discovered that their genetics is not a guarantee for an anxiety disorder, which is an indicator that the role of the environment in determining if you'll develop an anxiety disorderis very high.

There is some evidence which points to the fact that people can develop anxiety disorder from the environment alone.

It indicates that our life experiences go a long way in determining our mental health.

Some factors that cause anxiety includes;

Stress

Terrible life events can make an individual develop an anxiety disorder. However, the stress we encounter daily is one of the most common causes of anxiety. Long term stress in particular, like the one we experience in our 9-5 jobs or an emotionally abusive relationship appears to create anxiety disorder.

Anxiety and Stress have been known to have a pervasive link; it has been discovered that those that accumulate stress from how they live their daily lifeare likely to battle with anxiety for a longer time than those that have not experienced long term stress.

Some of the reason why stress causes anxiety is that;

- Stress tends to weaken the part of the brain that helps us control anxiety.

- Stress has a way of overwhelming the mind, thus affecting our ability to push the anxiety away.

- Stress may affect how we balance certain hormones, nutrition, and neurotransmitters.

A lot of people who suffered with panic attacks reported that their first panic attack happened during a period of stress like overcoming a breakup, a bad relationship, feeling overwhelmed in school, a bad job etc. PTSD has the name connotes is literally an anxiety disorder brought on by the trauma of experiencing a stressful event. This is furthercomplicated by the fact that stress has a way of creating itself. When stress weakens the part of the brain that helps you cope with anxiety, you will find it challenging to deal with anxiety in the future.

As a result of this, events that should naturally help you cope with stress will be a factor for you to be anxious. That is why those that say they were not under any stress when they first noticed their anxiety disorder may have still struggled to cope as a result of the past occurrence of stress.

To an extent, stress is the leading environmental factor that causes anxiety.

Life Experiences/Upbringing/Parenting

A lot of daily experiences shape the way you pattern your life, and a collection of those everyday experiences can prevent or promote an anxiety disorder.

- You can pick up anxiety from your parents (foster or biological),by watching how they reacted to circumstances when you were younger.

- You can create fear which leads to anxiety because of poor social interactions in your youth.

- If you were bullied in school or worried about classmates, school and teachers, it could cause you to develop anxiety.

Nearly every life experience works towards forging or preventing anxiety, sometimes in small and unnoticeable ways, while other times in many significant ways.

Trauma

Some traumatic experiences may lead to the development of anxiety disorders. Traumas can be defined as forms of severe and instant stress that is caused by certain external factors like sexual assault, neardeath experiences, witnessing the death of a loved one, violence and much more. Anxiety is very common in those with PTSD but it also predominant in individuals with panic disorder, generalized anxiety disorder, social phobia, and more. Trauma can affect you at any time after a traumatic incident occurred. Some children that have experienced some violence when they were youngonly developanxiety in adulthood. Trauma doesn't just cause anxiety, but it also has its ways of changing one's anxiety baseline. For example, if the person experiencesa lot of stress before the trauma, but theyhandleit well, and it doesn't lead to an anxiety disorder, the same amount of stress after the traumatic event can cause a severe anxiety disorder. Those who have experienced trauma are most likely going to have an anxiety disorder than those whohave not.

Change

A change in environment or circumstances can also lead to an anxiety disorder. Some people can quickly adapt to change, while otherscan't. These changes include some small changes like buying a new home,getting a new job, or some seemingly more massive changes like getting a divorce, the loss of a loved one, or a significant move.

Change puts people in an unfamiliar emotional state, and unfamiliarity can breed stress which can ultimately result in an anxiety disorder.

Abuse or Neglect

Although this can be categorisedunder trauma, we decided to give "abuse or neglect" a category of its own due to the sensitivity of the topic. Abuse and neglect can cause anxiety disorders in children and adults, it is well believed by many psychologists that a person's childhood is the sole creator of anxiety disorders that result from abuse or neglect, but realistically speaking, some form of abuse can occur to anybody at any age. For example, those in an emotionally damaging relationship usually find themselves suffering anxiety due to the emotional instability that this relationship creates. One of the responses that the mind of someone who has suffered from abuse or neglect can create is anxiety.

Anxiety caused by Anxiety

Anxiety can be sustaining and can re-occur because once you have it, the body begins to fear its re-occurrence then after a while, your body becomes accustomed to how it feels. Here are some other examples of how it happens;

- You may fear to ride a plane if you find yourself nervous about a plane ride.

- If you've had anxiety symptoms that were severe, you may be anxious about experiencing them again.

The principle behind this is that anxiety and a fear of anxiety symptoms can create more anxiety in the future. You can be led to a loop of anxiety as a result of the fear of the occurrence.

Anxiety Caused by Lifestyle Habits

The effect of your lifestyle in determining whether you have an anxiety disorder or not is very high, for example, research has proven that those who don't get adequate exercise are at risk of having an anxiety disorder. This happens because the body has unused energy and as such, it's not producing enough stresscoping hormones.

Similarly, your diet can play a role in determining if you have an anxiety disorder or not. For example, caffeine can exacerbate mild anxiety symptoms. You can also feel unhealthy when you consume unhealthy food, thus leading to stress which in turn causes anxiety. Even if you use a combination of medicine and therapy to fight your anxiety disorder, without a considerable change in lifestyle, you might not notice any improvement.

2.3.　The Negative Effects of Anxiety

Anxiety increases your heart rate and breathing in the short term, it directs blood flow to your brain where it's needed, and this physical response helps you to face an unwanted situation. However, if it gets too intense, it can make you feel nauseous and lightheaded. If anxiety becomes excessive and persistent, it can have a devastating effect on both your mental and physical health.

You can have an anxiety disorder at any point in your life. The symptoms of anxiety can stay hidden for a while,as such; don't wait till you get the sign before you embrace a lifestyle change, start immediately.

Anxiety disorder will affect your;

Central Nervous System

If you've had long-termanxiety anda series of panic attacks, it will make your brain release stress hormones more regularly than it should, this can increase the occurrence of some symptoms such as dizziness, headaches and depression. Some hormones and chemicals in your body are designed to help you cope with anxiety when you feel anxious your brain floods your nervous system with these chemicals and hormones. Examples of these chemicals are cortisol and adrenaline.

Cardiovascular system

If you have an anxiety disorder, you will consistently experience palpitations, rapid heart rate and chest pain all this may lead to an occurrence in high blood pressure and even heart disease. If you already have heart disease, and you then develop an anxiety disorder, your anxiety problem may raise the risk of coronary events.

Excretory and Digestive systems

This might seem too extreme, but it's true. Anxiety has a way of affecting your excretory and digestive systems. Some of the symptoms you'll notice are diarrhea, stomachaches, nausea and some other digestive issues. You can also experience loss of appetite occasionally.

Some connection has been noticed to exist between the development of irritable bowel syndrome (IBS) after a bowel infection and anxiety. IBS can lead to constipation, vomiting or diarrhea.

Immune System

Anxiety triggers your flightorfight stress response, which causes a flow of hormones and chemicals like adrenaline into your body system.

This influxof chemicals will increase your breathing and pulserate soyour brain can get more oxygen. This flow of chemicals and hormones prepares you to react well to an intense situation. It can make your immune system function better for a short while. Your body should come back to normal when you are in a calm environment. However, if you regularly feel anxious or the intense situation last for a long time, and your body never gets the sign to go back to its original state. If your body does not return to its original state, it can weaken your immune system, thus leaving you vulnerable to all type of infections. Your regularly vaccines may also not work well if you have an anxiety disorder.

Respiratory System

Anxiety can make you breathe rapidly and shallowly. If you have been diagnosed with chronic obstructive pulmonary disease (COPD), anxiety can land you in hospital due to anxietyrelated complications. Anxiety can also make symptoms of asthma worse.

2.4. How to Eliminate Anxiety

Anxiety disorder isn't an illness that you'll want to spend time managing; it's something that you should endeavour to find a way to eliminate. If you plan to learn how to eliminate your anxiety disorder, then read on. With hard work and enough dedication, you should solve the problem.

Mindful Breathing

You should realize that as much as anxiety is a mental health disorder, it is also a lifestyle problem. You need to be entirely concentrated in your fight against anxiety disorder, understand that your anxiety works like a prison system because it controls the way you think, and it can alter how much of your true potential that you fully express.

Anxiety is not something you can cure overnight. But once you're ready to embark on the journey till the end, no matter how long it takes, victory is yours.

Believing in the importance of curing your anxiety is very necessary; it will give you the motivation to continue. However, be careful about being anxious about fighting anxiety, that will lead you to the same problem you want to get away from.

Here are four mindful breathing exercises that can help reduce the occurrence of the symptom of an anxiety disorder.

A)   Inhale and Exhale

Here's how to perform the exercise;

- Close your eyes.

- Inhale and Exhale (breathe in as you usually do)

- Feel the air as it comes into your lungs, and feel the way you exhale, feel the whole action right to your spine.

- Observe the sensations around you, even your thoughts and the temperature of the environment.

- Inhale for fourseconds; hold your breath for seven seconds and exhale for eightseconds, do this repeatedly till you feel calm.

B)   Alternate Nostril Breathing Exercise

This exercise is also known as nadishodhana. The exercise is performed by inhaling through one nostril and using the other to exhale. The exercise might be short, but it is excellent for the brain as it helps in the steady flow of oxygen to both hemispheres of the brain. Practice this exercise every morning and more constantly when you want to do something new or worthwhile.

C) Ujjayi Breath

This exercise is known as so many names, some of which are hissing breath, victorious breath and ocean breath. The breathing exercise helps calm the mind from anxiety. It's an exercise that balances the mind, body and soul.

D) Lion's Breath

This is probably one of my best exercises, and I suggest that you do this exercise in an enclosed environment as you may look funny while doing it. Personally, it makes me feel like I'm letting go of all my worries. It will help you to release any emotion that might be a cause of your anxiety.

E) Grounding Technique for responding to panic attacks.

If you've suffered from any type of panic attack, do this exercise;

Breathe in and out slowly then look around and focus on;

- Five things you can see

- Four things you can hear

- Three things you can touch

- Two things you can smell

- One thing you can taste

Limit your alcohol intake

Alcohol can make you feel good, and I'm not saying that you shouldeliminate it completely.Alot of individuals use alcohol to relax after a busy day of work, but when taking alcohol, make sure that you drink sensibly. Research has proven that too much alcohol will give you anxiety rebound. Too much drinking also affectsyour sleep, and sleep is essential to managing an anxiety disorder.

Remove yourself from the anxious environment

When you're eager, the brain chemical "dopamine" gets activated, it sees the thing causing anxiety as a threat so it makes us feel uneasy. When you're anxious, instead of making that feeling swell up, channel that energy towards something else. You can excuse yourself to take a walk around the building or take a stroll to another section of the building or putsome water on your face to help you calm down.

Doing something that gets you away from the situation you're in will take the anxiety away.

Write down your anxious thought in a text

Instead of spending precious time thinking over a troubling idea, write those thoughts in the text message field and send it back to yourself. For example, you can say that "I'm worried aboutmy upcoming exam" or "I'm worried that I may not meet that deadline," then set a phone reminder to visit that thought at a convenient time.

What you've just done is that you've slowed down the thought that led to anxiety. When it is time to revisit that matter, you will be in a better mental state to address the issue. Any problem you solve in a state of anxiety would most likely lead to disaster.

Reduce your caffeine consumption

Caffeine, when taken in moderation, is not bad for your body. However, if you're anxious, caffeine can be a real anxiety trigger; this is because caffeine as a dosedependent affects your mood. A little quantity will perk you up, but too much of it will leave you irritable and anxious. Also, the sensitivity of every individual to caffeine differs. If you've been drinking multiple cups of caffeine before, try to reduce your intake and stick to one a day, then watch the positive effect that it will have on you.

Accept the fear

One of the most effective methods for tackling anxiety is accepting your fear for what it is. No matter the extent of your anxiety, whether it is extreme or mild, you have to accept your fear as one. It is after you accept it that you can tackle the demon.

Joseph Ruiz

Focus on the present

When you are feeling anxious about the future, try to force yourself to focus on the present moment. Focus on the beautiful dress you've got for the upcoming event rather than how you're going to be laughed at for being above average in weight. Focus on the current moment rather than what happened in the past.

CHAPTER 3

3.1. What is stress?

Stress is the way the body reacts to any change that requires a response or an adjustment. The body reacts to these changes mentally, emotionally, and physically. You can experience stress from your body, thoughts and your environment. Some positive life changes such as the birth of a child, a promotion, and a mortgage can produce stress.

3.2. What triggers stress in the body?

Stress is a natural occurrence that we experience while living our day to day activities, however despite it being what everyone experiences, what causes stress in an individual with similar lifestyle differs. For example, one person may feel angry with how a driver overtook him, while another may feel this same way in a severe traffic jam. Some may even turn up theirmusic while enjoying the beats while another individual present in this same atmosphere will experiencestress. A fight with a colleague might weigh someone down for several days, even weeks, while another may shrug it off quickly. In those scenarios described above, you will discover that what gives Mr A stress, may not give Mr B stress; as such, stress is unique to an individual.

What causes stress could be something you're aware of, but due to the nature of stress and the devastating effect that it can have on your physical, emotional, and mental health, you must keep an open mind to know what causes you stress. Craft your stress reduction strategy,keepingin mind all these factors.

Some of the factors that cause stress include;

Financial problems

Research has proven many times that the number one cause of stress for most individuals is money. It has been shown that over 50% of individuals around the world have stressed about money at least once every three months. The majority of those sampled revealed that over 50% feel considerably anxious about their finances. Signs of financial stress include;

- Arguing with loved ones about the distribution of funds.

- Feeling of guilt about how you spent money

- Anxiety about money

Financial stress can take some time to dispose of. However, the long-term stress from a financial problem can result in having high blood pressure, stomach upset, headaches, insomnia, chest pain and a general feeling of sickness. Financial stress has also been identifiedas the cause of many illnesses; some of those illnesses include anxiety, diabetes, arthritis, skin problems, and depression.

Work

According to a research done by the Centre for Disease Control and Prevention (CDC), average workers in the United States now spend 8% more time than at work than20 years ago, this statistic is not just true in the United States, but it also reflects what happens in different countries around the world. A lot of workers find their work very stressful.

A lot of things can contribute to job stress, some of which include dissatisfaction with a career or job, too much work, job insecurity, and conflict with a co-worker or boss. Whatever it is that causes you stress in your workplace, whether it is that annoying boss of yours, or that project with a deadline that is fast approaching, you should realize that putting work as your top priority can make other aspects of your life suffer. If you have a problem with other aspects of your life, it will inturn affect your ability to perform adequately in your work. As such, you may soon find yourself battling with a financial problem, which is another cause of stress.

Factors like an individual's psychological make-up, personal life, general health, and the amount of emotional support they receive outside work can also contribute to work stress. Signs that an individual is suffering from work stress include;

- Headache

- Anxiety

- Depression

- Heart palpitations

- Muscle tension and pain

- Fatigue

- Difficulty in making decisions and concentrating

When people struggle to cope with stress, it has a way to impact on their behaviour, and it may prompt individuals to experience a drop in productivity, disinterest, isolation, and a dropin work performance.

Personal Relationships

A lot of people that form some bond with us cause us stress, and it can be difficult to dissociate yourself from this source of stress. This stress can be from an intimate partner, family, co-worker or a friend. There are toxic people in many parts of our lives, and the stress we get from this set of people can harm our mental and personal health.

There are many reasons why couples can encounter stress in their relationship, and this stress can be the source of failure of the relationship. Some easily identified stressors are;

- Quality time becomes rare due to health problems, busy schedules or due to otherreasons.

- Lack of adequate communication between partners due to busy lifestyles

- Being too busy to spend eventful moments with each other.

- Abuse or a domineering attitude.

The signs of stress as a result of problems in your relationship are similar to what exists in general stress. Some of these symptoms are anxiety, sleep problems, depression, and physical health problems. You may also find out that you feel irritated by the individual that causes you stress.

Personal relationship stress can also be linked to our relationship with individuals on social media. For example, social media makes bullying easier, and it also gives room for comparison of lifestyle between an individual and the people theysee on social media.

Parenting

Parents are always faced with balancingextremely busyschedules; between training a child, building their future and trying tomeet their needs and expectations. These demands result in parenting stress.

A highlevel of parenting stress can make parents appear negative, harsh and excessively authoritative in their dealings with their children. Parenting stress also affects the quality of relationship you have with your child. For example, a high parenting stress level will not let you and your child have good quality interaction, which can make your child hide things from you and theywon'tcome to you for advice.

Some familiar sources of parenting stress include marital and relationship tension, lowincome, single parenting, working long hours, or raising a child that has a behaviour disorder or developmental disability. Numerous studies have shown that parents with children that have been diagnosed with autism have a higher level of parenting stress. This is also true of other behavioural disorders.

Daily Life and Busyness

Little inconveniences like misplacing keys, forgetting an important item at home, and running late are our day-to-day stressors that make stress accumulate into a mega problem. In most situations, these issues are just minor setbacks, but if they become more frequent, they can become a source of anxiety that will, in turn, have an effect on our psychological and/or physical health.

Studies have shown that the stress we get from being busy increases witheach passing year, in this modern time, people are workingmore than ever, and this adds some stress to our lives. Busyness, in most cases,is a result of some necessary needs that we need to meet. At other times it is due to not wanting to disappoint others and guilt. As a result of not wanting to disappoint others, some have an attitude of saying yes to everyone even at the detriment of their own psychological and physical health.

Personality and Resources

The resources available at your disposal and your personality trait can tie into all the factors described above and can even be an independent factor on its own.

For example, extroverts cope better with stress as they have great social resources which can help them to buffer the stress, while perfectionists may put unnecessary stress on themselves due to the standard they set for themselves which exacts negative health consequences.

3.3. How Stress Affects your Productivity

Stress is one of those factors that negatively impedes the productivity of any individual, as such, when stress creeps in, only a few can function to their full potential and this invariably leads to a drop in the individual's productivity, often affecting all those linked to the outcome of their work as a whole. Surprisingly, a sizeable amount of people feel that stress is a significant factor that affects their productivity; this demonstrates how big the issue is.

As difficult as this is to hear for supervisors, managers or even top-level employees, one factor that affects productivity is pressure which can also lead to stress. With stress being an increasing factor in reducing productivity in the workplace, it will be helpfulto recognise the damage that stress can cause in reducing productivity even with the most productive individual.

Joseph Ruiz

Stress;

Drains your Energy;

This might seemironic, but stress will give you a burst of adrenaline, that makes you extremely active for a while. However, you will feel a massive energy drain after that initial burst. You will soon find yourself feeling exhausted after a few hours when you're losing sleep, and you feel tired over stress, this phenomenon will not make you productive. Also, if the source of your stress is a relationship problem or some emotional distress, you will continuously find yourself being lost in thought, and this will affect your concentration, and invariably your productivity.

Wastes your time;

We've all at one time of our life spent time worrying on what we are stressed about, this can even lapse into the time we're meant to be working, and as such it will affect our productivity.

Causes interruptions

Have youbeen in that situationwhere you've had your internal fire alarm go off? When you're trying to get something important done,and you remember a vital stressinducing item that you forgot to do, this can make you drop what you're working on to sort things out.

Impairs your Judgement

Stress affects you in many ways than one; it can even cause you to do many things that you won't normally do. In some extreme cases, it can make people do some unethical things that they would not normally do.

Affects your personality

Stress directly affects your personality because you will be under an internally induced pressure, and this can make you express words harshly; it will also make you an angry individual. If you've ever had a supervisor at work that is under immense stress, you mayfindthemsnapping and yelling at others without knowing it.

Decreases your creativity

When you're stressed, you will have a problem with opening up and thinking of new ideas. This will make you latchon to the very first solution that comes to your mind.

Affects your relationship

It is the sad truth that a stressed individual often avoids interacting with others, whether it is your colleague at work, family and even friends. This is usually a a result of them being in a secluded world of their own with little ability to make small talks and polite discussions. Their inability to communicate adequately affects their productivity if they are occupying a position that requires that they communicate. The result will affect the individual a lot in the workplace. For example, they will not be able to communicate well or make pro-active suggestions at work meetings.

Absenteeism

Research conducted and published by the chartered institute of payroll professionals suggest that employees suffering from stress will mostlikely apply for daysoff due to sick days. Stress ranks among the most common causes of absence from the workplace. Those suffering from stress may find themselves suffering from symptoms such as a noticeable weight loss, headaches, difficulty sleeping, and high blood pressure.

These type of symptomscan take theretoll on the productivity of an individual, and those with nearperfect attendance will find themselves taking more time off work, thus reducing productivity.

Can Affect Staff Turnover

Virtually all companies have a small number of workers who from time to time struggle with timekeeping, the problem should become worrisome if individuals that are typically punctual start becoming sloppy with their timekeeping, even if it's by less than 5 minutes, it may be an indicator that stress is at play.

3.4 How Stress Affects Cognitive Thinking.

Cognition is the process of acquiring understanding and knowledge through the use of your senses, thoughts and experiences. Now that you understandwhat cognition means, you should ask yourself "Can I copewithout my cognition"? The answer is definitely no. Stress can impactour cognition as it affects our ability to think appropriately. Although stress is a common and familiar part of our daily life, and it happens in a variety of forms, we should be careful when stress begins to affect our capacity to reason.

Stress might come in a lot of forms; it might be the stress of trying to juggle school commitments, family and work. It can also involve issues like relationships, health and money. Whatever the form it takes or the issues involved, it can be the source of cognitive distortion

You have previously read abouthow stress can cause headaches and have a severe impact onour lives, part of how stress can affect our lives is by distortingour cognition, and it does this by affecting our brain. When stressed, your brain goes through a series of reactions, that is designed to mobilise and protect itself from perceived threats. Stress can also affect your brain positively as itcan help us to sharpen our minds and help us to improve our brain's ability to remember details about the event happening at that moment. Let's breakdownhow stress can affect our cognition;

Increases the Risk of Mental illness

Multiple pieces of research have proven that chronic stress causes a long term defect in the brain, it has been suggested that these changes are why those who experience chronic stress are at risk of anxiety disorder and excessive mood swings at a later stage of their life.

After a series of research done by the University of California-Berkeley, it was discovered that stress like thiscould create myelin-producing cells, but it also produces fewer neurons than you need. The result of this imbalance is that excess myelin in a certain part of the brain will interfere with the balance and timing of communication. It was also discovered that stress also affects your hippocampus, which is an essential part of the brain.

Stress Changes TheStructure Of The Brain

Chronic stress can cause a longterm change in the brain's function and structure. The brain contains a lot of support cells and neurons. These support cells are the ones that perform highorder thinking, such as problem-solving and decisionmaking. The brain also contains "white matter", which are axons that connect every region of the brain to communicate properly. The white matter was given that name because of the white sheath known as myelin that surrounds the axon whose responsibility is to speed electrical communication for faster communication between the brain; this is the reason why your brain can process information inan instant. Scientists have maintained that the primary reason why there can be an overproduction of myelin is a result of stress; this overproduction can also cause a lasting change in the brain.

Chronic stress will lead to aseries of problems that will affect your ability to reason; once the structure of the brain is changed, mental illness becomes inevitable.

Stress Kills Brain Cells

Research has discovered that a single socially stressing event can cause the death of new neurons in your hippocampus. It is one of the two areas discovered where you have the formation of a new brain cell.

Stress Hurts Your Memory

If you've ever had to remember something in a stressful environment, or you've had to write an exam or assessment test immediately after a stressful event, then you're probably aware of how stress can affect one's memory. Even, relatively minor stress can affect your ability to remember little things such as where you left your car keys, or where you kept your briefcase yesterday,at that moment when you're late for work.

The impact of stress on your memory can also affect some other variables like stress and memory retrieval.

Stress Shrinks The Brain

Stress can lead to brain shrinkage amongst both healthy and unhealthy people as it causes a decrease in the part of the brain that is responsible for *cognition,* metabolism and emotions.

Researchers have discovered that it is the everyday stress that we all face that causes the kind of stress that can affect our cognition rather than only those intense stress created by lifealtering events such as a car accident, a natural disaster orthe death of a loved one.

Chronic everyday stress in itself doesn't cause brain shrinkage, but it makes the brain susceptible to brain shrinkage when we are faced with traumatic and intense stressors.

It becomes difficult for an individual that has accumulated stress to solve problems that demand highlevel critical thinking skills to solve.

3.5. How Stress Affects your health

Stress can affect your health in more ways than you thought, some of which are;

AltersYour Hormones

During a stressful moment, your body issues several hormonal responses, the most common of those hormones which it responds with is cortisol. The cortisol is necessary for survival, as it plays a crucial role in your fight-or-flight response, it can be the survival factor at that moment where you're faced with death. However, overexposure to cortisol can lead toadverse healthproblems, some of which will be discussed later. Apart from the cortisol, stress also affects the thyroid hormone and even insulin. There have also been cases where chronic stress was identifiedas the cause of some endocrine disorders.

It Increases The Heart Rate

When you experiencestress,therate of your heartbeat increases; this is because stress causes the release of adrenaline, which inturn causes you to have a temporary spike in heart rate. This brief spike in heart rate is how your body increases the flow of blood through your entire body in case it is needed to react to a dangerous situation. Your body reacts as if some stressful situations are physically dangerous.

It Makes Breathing Difficult

Many physiological reactions are triggered by stress; one of those physiological reactions is muscle tension. This tension can affect the muscle in any part of your body, such as your chest and surrounding lungs. If this should ever happen, you may find it difficult to breathe, or you may experience a shortness of breath.

It Can Give You AHeadache

This is what medical doctors refer to as "tension headache," this type of headache is caused by stress, and it can vary in severity, it all depends on how intense the stress was. You can have an episodic headache after just one stressful event, but after a while of accumulating stress, you will have a chronic headache.

The physiological causes of headache vary, but it is often triggered by the tensed muscles at the head and the back of the neck.

It Can Worsen Your Memory

Irrespective of the number of brainboosting study snacks that you consume. If you are stressed about an incoming exam, it could affect your ability to remember what you have studied on your exam day. What could be worse than studying for an exam and not remembering what you read, you need to be careful of stress especially if you're studying for an exam or assessment, it has been proven that stress can result in reduced spatial memory and weaker verbal memory.

It Can Significantly Raise Your Blood Pressure

Stress has a twofold effect on your blood pressure; the short term effect on blood pressure and the long term effect. In the short term, stress hormones can cause your blood pressure to increase, but this is always a temporary increment. However, in the longer term, research has shown that stress can cause hypertension; this is because the repeated spike in hormones can increase the likelihood of lifelong high blood pressure. Also, some of those coping mechanisms that people turn to when they feel stressed have been known to be a massive cause of hypertension.

Some of those coping mechanism includes drinking alcohol, smoking cigarettes and neglecting sleep.

It Increases Your Chances Of Having A Stroke

In the United States, stroke is the leading cause of death, and stroke can be caused by stress. whenever you feel stressed, think of this fact, as such, it should make you take your stress reduction program seriously if you have one, and if you don't, you should enrol on one.

It Can Increase Your Chances Of Having A Heart Attack

There's a reason why the phrase "You almost gave me a heart attack exist" although you might find the phrase crass.

Your emotional stress increases the risk of you having a heart attack. According to a research done by the "American Institute of Stress," the coping mechanisms people use when stressed are huge factors that cause a heart attack, and records have shown that heart attacks tend to spike after a very stressful event like the death of a loved one.

An Increased risk of Type 2 Diabetes

Diabetes and stress are closely related, and this is because stress affects insulin, insulin is the chemical that helps to break down sugar in your body. It is when insulin cannot break down those sugar molecules that such an individual is diagnosed with diabetes.

It Upsets Your Stomach

Stress can leave you with some severe upset in your stomach. This happens because when there is a full flow of emotions triggered by stress, it can disrupt the movement in your bowels and digestive system in general, which can leave you with constipation, nausea, diarrhea, stomachaches and vomiting.

It can Lead ToAcid Reflux

It is not only food that triggers acid reflux, the sudden rush of hormones when your heart rate increases and other changes to your body system will increase your susceptibility to digestive distress.

Increase TheRisk of An Ulcer

The bacteria in the stomach called H. Pylori is the cause of ulcers and not stress, but stress can indirectly cause it because of the acidity change that can happen during these periods. If you have one, it can upset your ulcer.

It Can Cause Muscle Pain

Your muscles tense up in stressful situations; this happens to protect them from a potential injury that may occur. If it isshortterm stress, your muscles will relax to theoriginal position, but in a situation where it is chronic stress which is long term, chronic stress can further lead to chronic tension which can make you have muscle pain. When you have muscle pain, you don't have to rely on a pain reliever;

you should focus on preventing what caused the pain; this is the best way to approach the situation.

Increases The Risk ofCertain Infections

Research done by the American Institute of stress discovered that stress could increase the risk of infection in some male reproductive organs, e.g. the testes and prostate.

Disrupt Your Menstrual Cycle

Stress can disrupt the menstrual cycle of a woman. This disruption can show up as heavier or more painful periods, irregular periods, or missed periods. It is highly believed amongst many experts that the disruptive effect of stress is due to the cortisol that is released when you are stressed. This excess cortisol causes a chain reaction to occur in your hormones which then affects the hormone in the female reproductive cycle.

Weakens YourImmune System

Stress will affect your immune system positively in the short term. This is because of the fight-or-flight response which will trigger your immune system to act faster to heal any potential wound.

In the long-term, the effect of stress on your immune system ismore caustic. People who experience chronic stress daily have been known to have weaker immunity when compared to those who do not, what this means is that they will be very susceptible to all kinds of viral infections, from colds to more seriousinfections..

3.6. Types of Stress

To have a full grasp of what we're discussing, you have to understand the four types of stress that weexperience.Having anyof these types of stress on a repeated basis or for an extended period will result inyour body producing millions of free radicals, which can lead to free radical damage or oxidative stress, which can then cause you to have a severe chronic degenerative disease (CDDs).

There are over two hundred known CDD's that is caused by oxidative stress, of which about half are auto-immune diseases while the other half are inflammatory diseases.

These four types of stress perfectly complement the four main fields of stress (electromagnetic, chemical, emotional and physical) that exist. If you get stressed out continually in any of these fields, you need to work on it as it is hazardous.

The four types of stress are;

- Chronic eustress

- Acute eustress

- Acute distress

- Chronic distress

Let's explore each type of stress in more detail;

Chronic Eustress

Chronic eustress is a long-lasting, recurrent, good stress that is good for your body. This is the best type of stress, and it is at this point that your body is in its most productive state. This type of stress should be the type that everyone craves for. Although as desirable as this type of stress is, the body also needs a rest time from all types of stress. This level of stress puts you in a state where you're very aggressive, creative and consistent because this is where "real" productivity exists; however, don't forget that you need some time to wind down.

If things happen in life that pull you out of this state, that's goodbut make sure that you deal with the problem and return to this state as soon as you can because it is safer.

Free radicals can be created with every level of stress, so, be sure that you take steps to counter any free radicals being made by the body and replace these free radicals that are damaged.

This state has words like fun, peace, joy, happiness, fulfilment, love, spirit and laughter.The body feels very high levels of feelgood hormones like oxytocin, endorphins, dopamine and nitric oxide inthis state. These are the hormones that enable us to have a good and healthy relationship in every area of our lives, whether they are parental, work-related or romantic.

If you have been married for a long time and the feeling of newness and excitement seems to have gone in the wind, all you need to do is to get back into this level, and you will feel like you're falling in love all over again.

Acute Eustress

The second type of stress is known as acute eustress; it is that rapid onset, short, and intense good stress. If we're to create a 1-10 scale for types of stress with ten being good and one being bad, this type of stress will sit at about 6-7.

Anytime you get some fantastic good news, or something wonderful happens to you, or you are engaged in a work out that feels good, that is when you experience this type of stress.

Acute Distress

The third type of stress is called acute distress, and thisis a short, rapid onset and intensely bad stress. This type of stress happens when you feel threatened or shocked, and you get into the fight-or-flight mode. Your body sends out emergency response hormones like cortisol and adrenaline, which allows you to have a sudden boost in strength, prolonged endurance, and an increase in speed and energy.

You feel this type of stress during an accident, when you feel terrified or when you are attacked, it therefore allows us to respond to danger.

Although this type of stress is classified as bad stress, it is not that dangerous in the long term, provided that it is not overused, your body will flush out these extra hormones from the body.

This stress level usually leaves some extra cortisol in your body; you can flush out the excess cortisol following this acute stress with some great physical exercise which will allow you to flush out the extra cortisol faster.

Chronic Distress

This type of distress is a recurrent bad, longlasting stress, and it is the worst by every measurement, and sadly it is the most common. When the situation that produced this stress is left unsolved, the body starts to build-up free radicals at a rapid rate. Most problems traced to stress are as a result of thistype of stress. If you consistently suffer from this type of stress, your body will be pumped up with hormones like adrenaline and cortisol, and it will happen on a regular basis. When you overuse your endocrine system to a high extent, they will begin to malfunction, and that is a recipe for disaster.

The reason why there is a malfunction is that your endocrine was never designed by nature to release that high volume of hormones, not just that, but it is made to do so multiple times than it can handle. You should try your best to change the reason you're in this state, even if you have to change your job, ask for help, pray to a higher power, change your expectation if you need to, but you must do whatever it takes to get out of this level now and lead a happy and contented life.

3.7. Internal and External Causes of Stress

3.7.1. External Causes

There are varieties of external factors that can lead to stress. Some examples of stressors are;

Social stressors: Human communication and interaction can be a major factor that causes stress. Things that might stress youinclude what bosses, family members, co-workers, neighbors or even customer service representatives say or do. Also, happy events such as planning a party, preparing for a wedding, or having a baby can have the same negative effects on your stress levels.

Life-changing events: Unhappy events such as getting robbed, a job loss, house fire, accident, and the loss of a loved one can contribute to significant stress.

Demands of our daily life: Some daily routine activities such as paying your taxes, taking care of your kids, commuting to work can lead to accumulated stress. The social system that orders our activities also imposes deadlines, rules, regulations, useless meetings, unnecessary work, office politics, and non-stop emails all contribute to our stress levels.

Pushing Your Body Too hard: This is one of the significant sources of stress, over exerting yourself can be good, but only if done positively and in moderation, an example is exercise, but when it creeps into your daily activityand it becomes obsessive then it can become a stressor.An example of how not to push your body is when you spend too much time working; as such, it reduces the time you use to rest. Sooner or later, the constant energy drain causes your body to lag in its repair work. There won't be enough time to replace worn out neurotransmitters or fix damaged cells. Before you know it, changes will occur in the internal environment of your body, and this canlead to a physical illness like hypertension or even a stroke.

Environmental Factors: Extreme weather can cause stress. Very high altitude can cause stress as the oxygen supply at high altitude is low. Therefore,your cells won't be able to perform as effectively as they should. Poisons and toxins are also sources of stress. Each of the factors mentioned can cause a considerable amount of changes in your body

Tobacco Use

Tobacco is a very powerful toxin; it can destroy the cells that clean your lungs, trachea, and bronchi. Smoking is the number one cause of emphysema and chronic bronchitis, which can result in suffocation. If you smoke a cigarette or you stay around someone that smokes, you will inhale the carbon monoxide that comes from it, which can cause chronic carbon monoxide poisoning. Tobacco use can also create a reduction in the supply of blood to vital organs such as the brain and heart, and damage arteries in your body.

Chewing tobacco or snuff does not make you safer, it also has the same effect on your arteries, and it causes the same level of exposure to carcinogenic substances.

Causing physical illnesses like emphysema, cancer, chronic bronchitis, arterial damageare some of the factors that make tobacco a potent source of stress to life.

Allergic Stress

Allergies are an integral part of the body's defence mechanism when your body detects a substance that it considers toxic; your body will try to neutralize it, attract it or get rid of it. If the element is something that has found its way into your nose, you might get a runny nose. You might get blistering skin if it is something on your skin. If you inhale it, you might get wheezing in your lungs. If it is something you ate, it can cause the appearance of itchy red hives all over your body. Allergy is a cause of stress as it needs a considerable amount of energy to fight off a perceived threat to the body.

3.7.2. Internal Causes

Apart from those causes of stress that are from external circumstances, we can also create internal stress. We create stress internally when we worry, allow negative thought patterns to flow through our head, think negatively, set unrealistic deadlines for ourselves, or think of what others might think of us over our own feelings.

Those voices in our heads that give us unsolicited harmful advice are also another major factor that causes stress. An example of self-talk is when we tell ourselves that "look, the salesman is ignoring you, you should do something about it," this type of talk sometimes triggers stress within us.

Another type of stress is what experts call "anticipatory stress"; this occurs when you stress about things that might happen. Some of the events we worry over are those we have no control over. For example, you may stress about an upcomingfootball match, or a job interview.

Emotional Stress

This type of stress occurs due to disagreements, conflicts, and arguments.

Hormonal Factors

> Puberty: A lot of changes that occur in puberty can cause stress. During adolescence, the sexual organs begin to function, the body starts to change shape, new hormones are released, and these hormones can change our mood, especially when the body is just getting used to it.

> Pre-Menstrual Syndrome: A woman's body is designed to work best in the presence of some female hormones. When a woman passes the stage of puberty, the lack of female hormones can be a factor that causes stress in her. Once a month, the level of hormones that a woman has will fall

sharply; this sudden fall in hormone levels is enough to cause temporary overstress in the individual; this is what is called "Pre-menstrual syndrome (PMS)."

➢ Post-Partum: Women'shormone levels will change dramatically after pregnancy. Some women may experience over-stress as a result of the loss in pregnancy hormones.

➢ Menopause: Menopause is another stage in every woman's life when hormone levels decline, this decline in hormones happens slowly, neverthelessthis decline is sharp enough to cause stress tothe body.

If we look at the causes of stress as highlighted above, you will notice a lot of this happens to a lot of people, yet it is not everyone that encounters these stressors that become stressed; this shows that it is not the event itself that causes stress but our perception and how we react to those events. However, by having an understanding of what causes us stress, we can create solutions that lower our level of stress, by eliminating the causes if we can.

3.8. Identifying The Symptoms of Stress and Dealing With Them.

Every human has at one point, or the other felt like they're facing more than theycan handle, and this, amongst other things, is one of the primary sources of stress. Sometimes, you may be able to tell if you're under stress, and at other times, you might keep going without knowing the signs. Stress affects both your physical body and your emotional stability.

3.8.1.Symptoms of Stress

How you might feel;

- Impatient, aggressive or irritable

- Over-burdened

- Afraid, nervous or anxious

- Like your thoughts are racing out of control, and you can't switch them off

- Lonely or neglected

- Depressed

- Sense of disinterest in life

- Unable to enjoy yourself

How you might behave;

- Unable to concentrate

- Eating too little or too much

- Drinking alcohol or smoking more than usual

- Feelings of restlessness

- Picking at your skin

- Biting your nails

- Snapping at people

- Difficulty in making decisions

How you might be physically affected;

- Hyperventilating or shallow breathing

- Panic attacks

- Eyesore or blurred eyesight

- Difficulty in sleeping, nightmares or problem getting to sleep

- Sexual issues like lack of interest in sex, or inability to enjoy sex

- Tired all the time

- Clenching your jaw or grinding your teeth

- Chest pains

- Headaches

- Heartburn or indigestion

- Diarrhea or constipation

- Dizziness or fainting, feeling sick.

3.8.2. DealingWithStress Symptoms

Eventhough there are a lot of things that happen in your life daily that causes stress, there are lots of practical things that you can do to address the day-to-day stress that you encounter.

> ## ➢ **<u>Identify your triggers</u>**

You will be able to tackle stress better if you identify what triggers the problem. Identifying the triggers will help you to anticipate the issues and think of ways to solve them. Even if the situation is something you can't avoid, it will help if you can prepare yourself and expect the problem to occur.

It might surprise you to find out the number of things that you're trying to copewith at once. Have it in mind that being idle can causeas much stress as being too busy.

> ## ➢ **<u>Organize your time</u>**

Making some adjustments in your schedule can help you have better control of any tasks you're facing, and this will help you reduce the stress that emanates from that particular area.

- Identify your most active time of the dayand do your most important task of the day at that time. For example, if you're someone who works better at night, you should schedule those tasks that require top level concentration at night.

- Make a to-do list of your tasks. Arrange the tasks such that the most important ones will be the first on the list. Ask your supervisor or your manager to help you with your to-do list. You should push back the less important tasks when you're less stressed.

- Vary your activities. Balance the task you find difficult with the ones you enjoy doing.

- Try not to embark on so many activities together. You might find it challenging to do any significant tasks if you have too much on your mind. The thought of having too many tasks at one timecan overwhelm you, and this can bring on stress.

- Take things slowly and take breaks; doing this can make you more productive.

> **<u>Address some of the Causes</u>**

Some of the things that cause stress are things we can't do anything about, however there are still some practical ways to go about solving these types of problems. Accept what you can't change

Accepting what you can't change might not be an easy route, but sometimes, you have to admit that there are things you can't change. This step will help you focus your time and energy more productively.

➤ <u>**Make some lifestyle changes**</u>

Taking essential steps to look after your wellbeing can help you deal with stress. It can help you to reduce the impact of stress on your emotions and body.

- Practice being assertive and straightforward in communicating with others: Be prepared to say no when people make demands that are unrealistic from you.

- Use relaxation techniques: If you already know what makes you relax, make sure you set time aside to do it. Some activities that help people relax include listening to music, having a bath, or taking thedog for a walk.

- Develop your hobbies and interests: Doing an activity that is different from what causes you stress is a sensibleway to get away from stress. If you experiencefear as a result of over-thinking, you should try engaging in shared hobbies; it is a perfect way to feel relaxed.

- Make time for your friends: it might seem hard when you've got a lot of things on, but if you spend some time with your friends, it will help you get over the stress. Chatting with your friends can also help you to put things in perspective, and your opinion can also help them to relieve their stress. You also produce hormones that help you to reduce stress when you laugh with your friends.

- Find balance in your life: you may discover that a certain part of your life takes a predominant amount of time and energy. You should try channelling your attention to some other parts of your life like family, hobbies or friends, etc. to balance things out. Finding a balance in your life can help you to spread the pressure, and thus, it will relieve your stress.

➤ <u>Look after your physical health</u>

Take time to look after your physical health, as that will help you cope with the impact of stress; it will also help you to prevent illnesses as that itself is one of the factors that causes stress.. For example:

- Get a good sleep: stress can make it difficult to sleep, and this can cause sleep problems, which is known to be a cause of more complicated illnesses. Being well-rested also improves your ability to solve problems.

- Be more physically active: physical activity takes your mind off things that cause stress and as such, helps to downplay the effect of stress.

- Eat healthily: when you're stressed, you might be tempted to eat unnecessarily or eat too little. The type of food you eat can also affect how you feel.

➤ <u>Give yourself a break</u>

If you learn to give yourself a break and be kinder to yourself, it will help to reduce your stress levels.

- Reward yourself for achievements: celebrate when you have completed projects, even small things like making a decision or finishing a piece of work. You can reward yourself by treating yourself to a delicious meal, or telling yourself "well done."

- Get a change of scenery: Change your vicinity and take time away from your daily routine, even if it for just a few hours, it will make you feel better.

- Go on a holiday or take a break: Taking some type of break from your daily routine will help you to feel refreshed. Spend some time in an environment you admire; if you do, your body will refresh automatically.

- Resolve conflicts: resolve the dispute that is making you stressed, meet the person involved, and have a one on one discussion with them, this may be a difficult thing to do. If that is what you must do to feel better, then take the step.

- Forgive yourself: we all have that voice of blame in our heads, but the extent that we succumb to this voice can be a determinant in how we feel.

> ## <u>Use your support network</u>

Realize that whatever your source of stress is, you don't have to go through it alone. Some of your support networks could be;

- Family and friends: telling people close to you how you feel can be the whole difference in determining if your stress level is high or not. They may also be able to offer solutions to your source of stress.

- Support at work: at work, they could include your human resources department, line manager, union representative, or employee assistance schemes. Don't worry that your colleagues and bosses will see this as a weakness because your employers want you to be productive as well. If the environment in your workplace is not supportive, you should consider speaking to a trusted colleague at work.

- Support at college or university: at your place of study, they could include your tutors, student services, or student union.

- Online peer support: it will help if you can share what is causing you to stress with those with similar experiences, this can help you feel less alone.

- Your GP: if you feel like you need professional support, you should consider visiting a doctor; so that they can help you access treatments and check your overall health. They can also recommend that you take a break fromwork, college or university, and can send a note to your work that you need rest.

3.9. How Stress affects your personality

If you regularly expose yourself to stress, it can alter your nature and may even influence your moral behaviour. Stress affects our personality in lots of ways.

In general, the effect of stress on your personality happens in two stages:the short-term and long-term.

The long-term effect on your personality comes only after a long period of stress, and the result usually lasts long, while the short-term effect is typically instantaneous, and the result is generally short-lived (not in all cases).

Long-term exposure to stress can make you feel stressed and unsettled all the time. It might make you feel down all the timeand make you becomeanti-social.

<u>Short-term effect on your personality</u>

Your body prepares itself to respond to stress in the short run. It programs itself to focus only on the things it deems crucial; this makes your brain try to "automate" as much non-vital behaviour as possible. The effect of stress in shaping our personality is widespread, but only a few take cognizance of this change. For example, if you are spinning your pen in your hands while working or feeling sluggish, or smoking, exhibit introvert like behaviour because you don't have the strength to engage in discussion; these are some examples of the short-term effect of stress.

Personally, stress makes me withdraw from a gathering of people, and I avoid making the slightest contact with any individual; this is a habit my body has automatically programmed as a response to stress-filled activity and situations.

The long-term effect of stress on your personality

If you expose yourself to stress for an extended period, it can impact on your behaviour in one of the two following steps. Remember that the effect of stress on every individual's personality is not the same. It all depends on the individual and how he responds to the situation that is causing themstress.

If a constant stress trigger occurs in your body, and the situation is not well managed, then your stress in itself becomes a source of stress; this is because, after a while of being stressed, there will be an over-production of stress hormones and neurochemicals, which won't go away even if you remove the circumstances that led to stress in the first place.

This stage of stress is the most undesirable, and it can be very harmful; it is challenging to recognize and observe this type as it comes out of nowhere.

There are typical changes that you can look out for in your personality.

- Under-eating or over-eating

- Rapidspeaking

- An ill-temper, you will often get annoyed easily

- Chain-smoking

- Twisting your hair or touching your face constantly

- Sexual problems (loss of libido, tiredness, etc.)

Stress can make you feel tired all the time, even when you've done nothing physically or mentally taxing because your body may be unable to produce the stress hormones that will keep you going when you need to keep going. As such, it will alter your personality and make you extremely sluggish, both physically and mentally.

When you start noticing the short-term effect on your personality, it is a warning shot, approach a doctorimmediately for counselling and the necessary treatment.

CHAPTER 4

4.1. How Negative Thought Pattern can lead to Stress and Anxiety

Before you can tackle any psychological issue, you have to have a good understanding of it. To this end, I included this chapter to help you to understand negative thought patterns and how they can lead to stress and anxiety.

> ### All-or-Nothing Thinking

When you're caught up in a loop of negative thought patterns, if you fall short of a task or deadline, you will exaggerate the worst that could happen. This attitude will make you anxious about imaginary things, thus putting unnecessary pressure on yourself. You will begin to imagine all that could be lost from not doing this activity right, and as such, you will find it difficult to enjoy anything that you set your mind to do. For example, if you're playing tennis with your friends, you might be bothered so much about losing a match. Negative thinking will make events that are supposedly supposed to make you relax to be a source of stress for you.

To counter this cognitive distortion, counter it by being mindful of your activity. Decide to enjoy every supposedly unnecessary step that you take when performing a task. An example is focus on your company of friends, focus on the sport itself, and the gentleness of the breeze.

➢ <u>Overgeneralizing</u>

When negative thought patternstakehold, if one thing is going wrong, it can make you draw the general conclusion that everything else will go wrong. Or, if something unpleasant happens, you conclude and expect the re-occurrence of that unfortunate event.

I remember the very first time I took a flight, there was turbulence, and this made me overgeneralize this occurrence, thus affecting how I felt about taking an airplane. Whenever Igot a scheduled flight coming up, I became extremely anxious, and I imagined everything that could go wrong. This sort of assumption can result in a lot of unnecessary stress and anxiety,because the subsequent flight was calm, but I still felt anxious.

Here's another example. You had a bad relationship, and this affects your perception of how you seeother men orwomen. You then overgeneralize by telling yourself, "This will end just like the previous one."

➢ <u>Mentally Filtering Your Experience</u>

You filter out the positives of an event, and you dwell on the disappointments and the negatives. If you do this continuously, it can lead to unnecessary stress and anxiety. Whether you're chronically ill or not, your life experiences should be a mixture of positives and negatives, pressure can occasionally occur in everyone's life, but if you dwell only on the ills of life, it is the perfect recipe for chronic stress.

➢ <u>Disqualifying The Positive</u>

Here, you won't just be ignoring the positive and focusing on the negative, but you will also turn those positive experiences into negative ones. You will fret over positive experiences because of your perception ofthem. For example, if you get a call from a friend, you will begin to imagine things like, "She's only calling me because she needs something from me." Disqualifying the positive can affect your stress levels as you won't derive joy from events should make youhappy. A surprise birthday party for you becomes a stressful exercise because you suspect the motive behind it.

➢ <u>Jumping To Conclusions</u>

Jumping to conclusions is also known as "mind-reading" error. It happens when you make a wrong assumption and conclusion about an issue without subsequent evidence to back them up You can conclude that someone has a negative thought towards you, while that person is just having a terrible day.

Let me give you an example that has probably happened to a lot of us, here's a typical example, have you ever passed beside someone, and you hear the person laugh? You may have that feeling that the individual is laughing at you while theyjust found something funny on theirphone, or remembered an entertaining event.

➢ <u>**Catastrophizing (also known as Magnifying)**</u>

Catastrophizing occurs when you exaggerate an unwanted situation, the occurrence of an undesirablecondition or you magnify what someone said or how they feel about you. You can compare it to looking at something through a binocular, which blows it all out of proportion. For example, I once thought that I had a severe medical condition, I searched for the symptoms of the sickness on the internet, and surprisingly, I started manifesting the signs, it wasn't until I went to the hospital and theydid a medical checkup that I feltbetter. What happened here is that I magnified my headache and linked it with something I had done, then I started imagining that I had developed another illness. This phenomenon is called *illness anxiety disorder,* and it is a result of negative thinking. When you have this disorder, you worry, and this will put you under unnecessary stress.

I'd be stunned if anyone reading this bookhas not suffered from this disorder at one point or the other in their life. This attitude can put an individual under enormous stress if they are not checked by a medical professional.

➢ <u>**Relying on Emotional Reasoning**</u>

This negative thought pattern can make you be really harsh to yourself. "I feel like a failure at building a home; therefore, I am a failure." "I feel stupid because I can't figure out where my life's headed; therefore, I am stupid. "I feel as if I was boring on that date; therefore, I am boring." These harsh words to ourselves fuels stress in us.

4.2. How ToUse Positive Affirmations To Deal With Stress And Anxiety

Whether you're giving an important presentation or you're attending a party alone, there are numerous ways and conditions where negative thoughts can creep up onus. Whether you have anxiety disorder or stress is getting toyou, fears and negativity can distract an individual faster than anything else, thus leading you to a downward spiral of emotions. For you to declutter your mind of all this, you need to master how to swap negativity with positive, rational thoughts. You will gradually start getting used to these positive thoughts, the more you practice, and this will eventually shape your thinking habits and will help you to strive faster towards the new you. Here are ways to use positive affirmations to deal with anxiety and stress.

> ➤ **<u>Identify and Stop Those Negative Thoughts</u>**

You need to learn how to identify negative thoughts so that you can get rid of those thoughts the moment you notice them in your mind. For example, if you say, "I feel like a failure at building a home; therefore, I am a failure." Identify that thought as a negative oneand get rid of it that very moment. Intentionally decide to refocus how you think, from negativity to a more positive one. Remind yourself that you're trying your best, and everything will probably turn out well. Do not wrap your thoughts around those negative feelings.

➤ <u>**Continuously Use Positive Affirmations**</u>

It will be very helpful if you canlearn some positive affirmations ahead of that stressful moment and when you can't seem to get rid of your anxiety. Consider the options below for common scenarios.

When faced with a situation that generates stress and anxiety, such as being overwhelmed at work, meeting new people or travelling, repeat those affirmations that you've mastered, and repeat them till you momentarily feel better at the moment. Make sure that those affirmations acknowledge your negative emotions and thoughts. Some examples include;Stress is dangerous; I need to get myself off work now.

- The picture that I have in my head will make me stressed and anxious. It isn't healthy. That's just me being cynical.

- I will be okay.

- I need to rest. If not, I am attracting undesirable diseases.

- I will focus on my hobbies to get me through this.

It can be challenging to manage your anxiety and stress, especially in times when you're in the spotlight like when you need to give a presentation or make a speech, in a situation like that, your disorder might tempt you to call insick. Don't! While stress requires that you take a break,you don't want to breakdown with a more severe sickness.

- If I keep going, I may never get anything out of it as I can breakdown.

- The last time I presented, my bosses were impressed

- If I take deep breaths, that will make me feel calm as I go in.

➢ **Remain Realistic**

Be careful of being unrealistic with your affirmations. If it is not realistic, you won't believe what you're saying, and if you doubt those words, the exercise becomes futile. Unrealistic positive affirmations can trigger more anxiety because your mind begins to tell you that your ideas are silly. If you start saying to yourself that you can do what you don't have a capacity for, it can make your stress levels increase, and the reality of failure hits hard.

When you want to write your positive affirmation, follow the examples above.

4.3. Identifying the Root Causes of Negative Thoughts

Negative thoughts come and go throughout the day, but when these thoughts linger for a long time, it becomes the cause of many illnesses. Our lifedepends on the extent to which we accommodate negative thoughts. You can accept these thoughts, ignore them, confront them headon or in a logical way.If you let these thoughts get to you, it can really damage your mental stateand affect your self-worth if you allow them to. Negative thoughts can limit how much potential we fulfil.

Here are three roots causes of Negative thoughts;

> ## **Fear of the future**

It is human nature to fear the unknown and the unpredictable. People have tried to predict the future by looking at the palm, staring at a globe or mixing some things together, observing the flight of birds by throwing bones or sticks on the ground, whether these work are not our focus, but we know for a fact that the fear of the future is what drives the majority of these actions.

People want to know what the futureholds, will it bring happiness? Or sadness? Science has made advancements in its ability to predict the occurrence of an action in the short-term in a closed system like the weather or elections. But most people worry about what the future will bring and how things will turn out for them in the short and long term.

Many people expect that their wishes for the future will happen just by wishing. We waste valuable time imagining what could go wrong about a future we have no control over; it's like paying interest on a credit card that you haven't used.

The fear of the future is a result of a perceived lack of control over what we hold dear to us. One of the best ways to predict the future it took make realistic plans for the future and follow it through. If you make a step-by-step plan for your wants, you can have some level of control over it.

Write down some small and realistic short-term goals that fit into your plans for the future. Planning will help you to reduce the number of negative thoughts that pop-up in your head and, consequentially, the fear of the future.

> **Anxiety about the present**

There are so many sources of worry that make an average person anxious about the present. We worry about things at work, about whether our kids made it to school, whether we locked the house door, or whether we will meet the deadline.

The easiest way not to be anxious about the present is by creating a to-do list for the day before you start in the morning. You can make one for your house so that everyone knows what they need to do and how important they are to you. Delegate responsibilities to those you know are capable only, if you delegate to the wrong person, that in itself can be a source of anxiety.

> **Shame in your Past**

Everyone has done things thatthey are not proud of, but some get over thispity overtime, while others can't seem to get over this shame. The thought of that period of shame often bubbles up on occasions.

CHAPTER 5

5.1. The Power of Emotions

An emotion is a strong feeling of sadness, joy, anger, or fear that moves us. The experience of these emotions is what makes you enjoy living. It is what transforms our life from a series of facts and dull tasteless events into a living and breathing experience. How you feel affects your energy, heart rhythms, relations, thoughts, and entire body;it is usually a difficult task to think right when we have emotions of anger or sadness. It doesn't make us choose wisely and behave appropriately,and this attitude makes us regret an inevitable consequence. Also, when you feel secure, cared for, appreciated, and joyful, your heart rhythms will be smooth and even. They send positive signals to your brain, making it think right and helps to make quick decisions.

To succeed in life, it takes more than intellectual and technical proficiency alone. It is highly sacrosanct to know how to manage your emotions. Instead of letting your feelings knock you over, you have to learn to ride the waves.Your brain consists of three parts; the first part drives your reflexes, instincts, and essential physical functions. The second part drives your emotions and feelings. It is the part that guides what you like and dislike. It is responsible for storing your memory and what you learned from your past mistakes. It helps you to remember the past, but it can't calculate risks, foresee the future, or consider the consequences of your actions. The third part of the brain is responsible for solving a problem. It protects you from those impulsive responses of the second part of the second brain. If you learn how to use the three parts of your brain harmoniously, you can achieve great things.

Your emotion is the power of your mind, and it influences your energy. Although all thoughts fuel ourstrength to some extent, emotions are very instrumental in determining what comes into our lives, and our physical realities are sometimes a product of our feelings. When we charge our thoughts with our beliefs, it can become a potent tool for leaping over any hindrance on our path to success, as long as you are aware of the fact that you can use the emotions in your life for any purpose.

5.2. How to Develop Positive Emotions

In much personal growth advice, you will notice that the focal point is usually on positive emotions; this is because your emotional development is the most integral part of your personal development.

We think to ourselves, "I'm going to make this decision that will make me more productive, more outgoing and more optimistic" and of course there's nothing wrong with this mindset; there are probably many techniques that can help you with these goals. However, the best way to achieve this goal would probably elude you because the answer is so simple that a lot of us don't set our minds on it. It turns out that the most efficient way of developing positive emotions is by having positive emotions.

The idea that initiated this thought pattern came from psychology. This reasonably simple assumption is called broaden and build theory, and it argues that "negative emotion leads to more negative emotions."

Due to how our brain is made to function, negative emotion makes us focus on only our safety, and physiological needs as such our reasoning is limited.

> ## **<u>Positive emotions lead to more feelings</u>**

Positive emotions work in the same way as a negative emotion, but the results are a world apart.

What happens when we experience positive emotions is that the horizon of our mind expands, our brains lose that narrow focus, and we experience those wild and explorative thoughts which encourage us to take the bold steps that matter. Positive emotions can build on themselves; as such, when you experience positive emotions, it can create a chain of more positive emotions and gives us a broader view of the scope of things. When we build up positive emotions, it can have a remarkably positive effect on different aspects of our lives.

<u>FourWays To Develop Positive Emotions</u>

Numerous techniques can help you to bring positive emotions into your life. Here are some;

> ## **Relaxation Techniques**

Some common relaxation technique includes the likes of yoga, meditation, and muscle relaxation exercises. Contentment is an essential emotion you should have when using any relaxation technique; it is a useful tool for building resilience to negative emotions and reversing the effect of those negative emotions.

> ## **Find Positive Meaning: this technique works in three ways:**

- -By reframing the adverse situation in a more positive way (positive reappraisal)

- -Adding positive values to events that seem ordinary

- -It helps you to pursue and aim toward realistic goals.

If you want to find a more positive meaning in your life, you have to be conscious of it. Evaluate the situation you're in and try to apply those three techniques above. One significant benefit of finding positive meaning in your life is that people with a lot of positive purpose in their life will experience a widerrange of positive emotions.

> Just Smile: our brains don't know the difference when we fake a smile and when the smile is real as such, the two trigger the same hormone in us. So, if you have no positive emotion that you can focus your mind on, just fake a smile.

> ➢ Do something you love: find the things you love to do and give time to doing them. Those things will make you feel good and relax.

5.3. How to Use Positive Emotions to Grow

Emotional IQ and soft skills have become the buzzword in the corporate world because employers have realized that positive emotions are fundamental to have dedicated and productive staff in these following areas:

- Teamwork

- Engagement

- Corporate strategy

- Decision making

- Attitudes

- Workplace satisfaction

- Customer service

- Innovation

- Health and safety

- An organization's financial performance

When it comes to development, experts have proven that positive emotions are vital for understanding and quick assimilation. When you use positive emotions in every area of your life, you will gain emotional resilience and will be able to do things more productively. Negativity can hinder your ability to reason, and as such, learning will be difficult for a student. People who are uncomfortable, fearful, or anxious cannot learn.

5.4. Letting go of Negative Emotions that Leads to Stress and Anxiety

Life will give you bad moments now, and then, that is the order of things, and when those bad emotionsdisappear, we grow from them and enter into another phase ofour lives. However, as much as these terrible situations are, they are lessons for us to get better. We still have the tough job of dealing with the emotions that these bad moments produce. Our instincts tell us to bury these feelings and hide from them, but that won't solve the problem as those feelings can appear at anytime, when triggered by different occurences.Your mind is always trying its best to keep itself from discomfort, which is why it is so much more comforting to hide from what causes us anger, remorse, anxiety, stress, and grief. But putting off these feelings only results in chronic distress which makes us suffer for longer just because we cannot summon up the courage, we need to tackle those negative emotions that cause us anxiety and stress.

But how do we summon up some courage to fight those emotions that lead to stress and anxiety? Think of it like this: rather than covering those emotions you don't want to confront, slowly turn your attention towards the cause of the problem, you don't necessarily have to look at it head-on, but don't avoid the emotions altogether. Don't just deal with the pain, also tackle the cause. Here is a six-step process that can help you to let go of those negative emotions that lead to stress and anxiety.

> ### **Pause And Return**

When we arehit by anxiety and stress, our instinct tells us to run away and shield ourselves from those bad emotions. But coming to terms with those emotions is the most crucial part of recovery. If you turn away from those bad emotions, you will never begin the recovery process because you will never really allow yourself to experience the inevitable. So, stop the instinctive reaction to hide from your emotions and face your fears. Get this done as soon as possible and begin the next step, the sooner you come to understand your feelings, the faster you will get out of there "shackles."

> ### **Identify Every Side of the Negativity**

You have to tell the truth to yourself. You must see negativity forwhat it is. Whether it as a result of embarrassment, pain, hatred, or shame. You must see it for its actual self. Convincing yourself that it's not as dangerous as it might be is still hiding from the negative emotions. If there is worry inside you, say it to yourself immediately, "worry exists within me, and I acknowledge that." If you have done something shameful, recognize it as the cause of your stress, rather than mask them as what they are not.

➢ **Accept**

Once you've identified those negative emotions as what they are, accept that the cause of this emotion is something beyond your reach, and there is nothing you can do about it. You should set some time aside and admit to yourself that you recognize the negative emotions inside of you, why they are there, and you cannot reverse this condition.

➢ **Realize that nothing lasts forever**

Negative emotions are stronger than positive ones. They are challenging to get rid of as they stick to us for a long time, even permanently if not dealt with, and they have a more significant impact on us. But what you should realize is that they will not last forever as long as you're taking significant steps to correctthem, some even disappear forever on thereown. For example, try to think of your worst memories, now ask yourself how you feel about that memory, and compare your feelings than with how you feel now. You will notice that these memories are somewhat vague, andnot as intense as how you felt in the heat of the moment.

➢ **Self-reflect on what has happened and respond**

A lot of people trap themselves in the downward spiral of emotional negativity, and all these emotions lead to stress and anxiety, all they need is a little push, if it has not led to stress and anxiety already.

When one bad thing happens, instead of responding sanely, they lash out in negativity, and they act rashly, thus causing more bad things to occur.

Reflect on the situation that is making you anxious and think about the best and least stressful way to get out of the mess with your dignity intact.

> ## **Be open to the future**

The last step of getting rid of negative emotion is pretty simple: don't fear the future. Accept that you don't have complete influence over what the future holds, present, and the positive emotions determine your destiny. Be happy and decide to work towards your goals.

CHAPTER 6

6.1. Stress Management and Relaxation

To tackle stress effectively, you have to activate the natural relaxation response of your body. Some relaxation techniques, such as visualization, meditation, yoga, anddeep breathing can help.

Finding the best relaxation technique that works for you

Relaxation for a lot of us means flopping on the couch and watching the TV for the rest of the day. But this is not effective enough to reduce the damaging effect of stress. Instead, you should work on activating your body's natural relaxation response. When you do this, you will enter a state of deep rest that lowers your blood pressure, slows your heart and breathing rate, brings your mind and body back into a balance, and puts the brakes on stress. Some relaxation techniques such as rhythmic exercise, meditation, deep breathing, yoga, or tai chi can get you to that state of rest.

It's imperative to know that there is no single relaxation technique that works for everybody. You have to discover what works for you and stick to it. The one that works for you is the technique that can focus your mind on bringing out your inner relaxation response and fits your lifestyle. Finding the right relaxation technique may require some trial and error. Once you've identified it, practice regularly, and you should experience a reduction in anxiety and stress, it will also boost your mood and energy, improve your sleep, and improve your overall wellbeing. Let's discuss some relaxation techniques that can help you relieve stress.

1. Deep Breathing:

This powerful relaxation technique is straightforward yet also comfortable. It's a technique that can be practiced anywhere and at anytime.It is easy to learn, and it provides a fast way to reduce your stress levels. Many relaxation practices depend on this technique, and you can do this with some other relaxation techniques such as music and aromatherapy. All you need to practice deep breathing is a few minutes and a quiet place to sit and stretch.

How To Practice Deep Breathing

- With your back straight, sit comfortably and place your hand on your chest, while you put the other on your stomach.

- Breathe in through your nostrils. While you do this, the hand on your stomach should rise, and the one on your chest should move a bit.

- Exhale through your mouth, while doing that, push out as much air as you can while you contract the muscles in your stomach. The hand you put on your stomach should move in, but your other hand should not move much.

- Continue the process of breathing in through your nose and breathing out through your mouth. Try inhaling enough so that your lower abdomen falls and rises. While you exhale, count slowly.

If breathing from your stomach while sitting up is not comfortable, you can breathe lying down. Put a flat object on your stomach so that the object falls as you exhale and rises as you inhale.

2. Progressive Muscle Relaxation

Progressive muscle relaxation technique is a two-step process where you relax and tense different muscle groups in your body. If you practice it regularly, it will help you to be familiar with how your body feels when you're in a relaxation moodor when it's tense. Once you identify these two, you can then identify and react to the first signs of the muscular tension that goes with stress. Your mind will relax as your body relaxes. You can combine progressive muscle relaxation with deep breathing if you're suffering from chronic stress.

Practicing Progressive Muscle Relaxation

If you have a history of the following; back problems, muscle spasms, or other serious injuries that may be aggravated by tensing muscles, then you should first consult your doctor.

Start tensing and relaxing the muscles of your feet first, then gradually work your way up to your face. Try to tense only those muscles you want to. Here's how to go about it;

- Take off your and shoes, your clothing, and any other things that might preventyou from being comfortable.

- In a calm mood, take a few minutes to breathe in and out slowly, let those breaths be deep.

- When you're ready to start, shift your attention to your right foot and be mindful of how it feels.

- Tense your right foot muscles slowly, tense as tight as you can. Hold for about 10 seconds.

- Remain in a calm state for a moment, breathing slowly and deeply.

- Move to your left foot and do the same.

- Shift your attention to adifferent muscle group inyour body, contract, and relax each of those muscle groups.

- It may take a while to know how to tense targeted muscles, take your time to learn it.

Muscle relaxation sequence

- Right foot, then to the left foot.

- Right calf and then move to the left one.

- Right,then, left calf.

- Stomach

- Chest

- Back

- Your right arm and hand, then shift your attention to your left arm and hand.

- Your neck and shoulders.

- Face.

3. Body Scan Meditation

Body scan meditation is a technique for relaxing that focuses your attention on different parts of your body. Just like progressive muscle relaxation where you start from your feet, then work your way up to other parts of your body. But rather than tensing and relaxing the muscles on those parts of your body, you focus on how your body feels on each part of it without labeling itas good or bad.

- Lie on your back, cross your legs, relax your arms at your side, and close or open your eyes, whichever suits you. Focus your attention on the way you breathe for about three minutes until you start feeling calm.

- Focus on the toes on your right foot. Pay attention to all the sensations you feel and continue to focus on your breathing. Imagine that each deep breath flows into each toe. Let your focus be on your toes for six seconds.

- Focus your attention to your right foot's sole. Feel the sensations in that part of the body and imagine the way each breath flows to the bottom of your foot. After a few minutes, shift your attention to the right ankle and repeat the process. Move to other parts of your body like your calf, torso, thigh, hip, etc. if there is any part of your body that causes you discomfort or pain, pay attention to that part.

- Once you have completed the body scan, relax and stretch if you feel the need.

4. Visualization (Guided imagery)

This technique involves imagininga scene that lets go of all tension and anxiety and makes you feel at peace. Choose whatever setting that makes you feel calm; it could be a favorite childhood spot, tropical beach or a quiet wooded glen.

You can practice the technique with the help of a personal guide or listening aids or on your own. Here's how to practice visualization if you imagine a tropical beach.

Private Visualization

Close your eyes tightly and imagine yourself in a peaceful and calm place. Let your picture of the site be as vivid as you can: everything you smell, taste, feel, and hear.

Visualization won't work well if you don't incorporate as many sensory details as possible. For example, if your restful place is a dock on a quiet lake:

- Imagine the sun setting over the water

- Hear the birds sing.

- Feel the cool breeze touching your body.

- Feel the fresh air.

- If you pay attention to the correct parts of your body, you will feel as though your worries drift away as your body gradually feels calm. You might lose track sometimes, that's perfectly normal. Continue from where you were as soon as possible.

5. <u>Rhythmic movement and mindful exercise</u>

The idea of engaging in an activity like this might not sound soothing, but rhythmic activities that put you in a flow of repetitive action can make you feel relaxed. Examples include:

- Walking.

- Dancing.

- Swimming.

- Rowing.

- Climbing.

For a perfect result, add mindfulness to your workout.

Adding mindfulness to your rhythmic exercise will be more beneficial to you than only a rhythmic movement. Mindfulness will shift your focus from your daily concerns and worries about how your body feels right now. Focus on how your breath complements how you move and the sensations in your limbs. For example, if you're running, focus on how your sole feels as your feet touch the ground.

6.2. How to Effectively Manage Stress and Anxiety

Stress and anxiety are a normal occurrence in everyday life. Everyone experiences stress and anxiety, although on different levels. However, when this problem reaches the level where it hampers our productivity and how we live our daily lives, then we need to get rid of the problem as it can lead to emotional, mental, and physical breakdown. Learning how to manage our stress and anxiety can be what determines whether we'll reach our goals or not.

Here are some easy and simple practices you can do to help you manage those feelings of negative stress and anxiety disorder.

1.Yoga

Yoga can help you feel calm when you feel anxious or after a stressful day. Although many people consider yoga as an exercise, it can give the mind a relaxing experience.

When to take a Yoga class

- When you want to relieve stress in your body

- When you need to stay present at the moment.

2. Meditation

Meditation is a very effective way to release anxiety and stress and to keep negative emotions at bay. The time you allocate as your meditation period doesn't have to be much. If you can spare a few minutes daily, you can meditate. Many people feel that they have to do it for some hours and keep their mind blank, which is not valid. You can meditate while typing or jogging.

3. Self-Massage

You probably know how effective massage is in fighting stress and anxiety. However, self-massage produces the same result. Take some minutes off work to massage yourself. It could be those few free minutes between tasks or on the couch after a hectic day.To enhance the experience, you can use scented lotion, aromatic oil, or a combinationof self-massage or deep breathing exercises.

Self-massage

- Knead the muscles on your shoulders and at the back of your neck. Make a loose fist and drum the sides and back swiftly. After that, move your thumb in a circular motion around the base of your skull. Massage the rest of your scalp slowly, then tap your scalp with your fingers gently moving in a front to back motion and then sideways.

- Massage your face: use your fingertips or your thumb to massage your jaw muscles, temples, and forehead. Massage the bridge of your nose through your eyebrows to your temples.

- Close your eyes and cup your hand loosely over your face, then inhale and exhale for some seconds.

Other Benefits of Self-Massage

- It raises the level of serotonin and oxytocin in the body; these two chemicals are known to reduce the level of stress in the body.

- It reduces your blood pressure because it enhances the relaxation response.

- It helps people sleep better.

4. Breathing

Breathing can also help us reduce stress, and this type of breathing is called mindful breathing. With this breathing technique, you can purposefully change how you feel, how your body reacts to what's going on around you, and even the way you breathe in and out.

Benefits of breathing exercises

- It will make you feel more relaxed, less anxious, and tense.

- Make you feel calm.

- It forces your mind off your worry.

<u>Types of breathing exercises</u>

Counting breaths-: Breathe in deeply and out counting to one. Take another deep breath, then exhale and number two. Continue this untilyou reach ten.

Belly Breathing-: Let your focus be on how your stomachfills with air when you breathe through your nose. Breathe in and notice your stomach expand, then breathe out and feel it contrast when you exhale. Continue untilyour focus is totally on this action.

4-7-8 Breathing: Breathe in and count four, hold your breath and count seven, then exhale gradually while counting eight.

6.3. Using Cognitive Therapy to Deal with Stress and Anxiety

Cognitive therapy can help you if you have problems where changing your thoughts and beliefs are crucial, like anxiety and stress. Whether your anxiety or stress is affecting how you live your daily life or is just creating those unpleasant feelings, cognitive therapy is a very efficient mode of treatment.

Cognitive therapy for anxiety and stress rests on the theory that it's not the events that cause us stress and anxiety; it's our perception about them and how you react to them.

There are over a hundred examples of why it is our perception and reaction about an event and not the situation that causes stress. For example, two people might be stuck in traffic, while one may have a high-stress level as a result of the event, the other may see it as the time to listen to that audio-book theygot on Amazon or get lost in funny thoughts.

Therapists use cognitive therapy to alter your thought patterns and reduce your level of stress and anxiety.

Many people find cognitive therapy to be more helpful than most therapeutic approaches. In most cases where experts use cognitive therapy to treat anxiety and stress, there is usually a noticeable improvement within four to five weeks; this is faster than psychoanalytic treatment, which can take years before you notice any significant improvement. An example of Cognitive therapy is *Thought Records*.

Thought Diaries/Thought Records

This method is a straightforward method for addressing negative thinking and emotions that cause anxiety and stress. In this technique, the psychologists involved will ask you to write down your negative thoughts that led to your stress and anxiety (e.g. My boss will fire me if the presentation is not right, I am a failure, I suck at being a father, etc.), the situation in which this thought came to your mind (e.g. talking with a colleague at work), and the emotions you felt at that moment (e.g. worry, anxiety), what you did to cope with the situation and the outcome.

This technique is perfect for identifying the root cause of your stress and anxiety and recommending the right method to help you get over those negativities and situations.

CHAPTER 7

7.1. How to Declutter Your Mind and Achieve your Goals

A mind that is cluttered is indecisive, unproductive, and stuck in its way. It is necessary to get rid of this clutter, just as much as you would do to your physical clutter, as it helps you to concentrate on your goals and make way for things you deem essential. Below is a three-step process that will help you to get rid of any mental clutter that can prevent you from achieving your goals.

1. Be Decisive

When you know what you want, achieving your set goals becomes easier to achieve than most people think. Every day, we face a plethora of problems that demand that we make decisions that will get us closer to our goals or farther from them. What should be the agenda for next week's meeting? Should I register for that course? What should I write in that e-mail? When should I approach that investor? What should I do about my marriage?

You have so much on your mind, and making a decision seems like something too enormous, but the more you delay in making that decision, the more you find it challenging to achieve your goals. According to numerous researchers, "the reason why most people are not decisive in making decisions that will drive them towards their goals, is not that they do not know the right decision to take, but due to the fear of making the wrong one."

Being decisive is one vital way to declutter your mind. So, stop worrying and start taking the right steps. Evaluate the pros and cons of every choice that you have and make the right step without looking back.

Prioritize

Make your goals clearerand make a to-do list of what you want to do each day/week/month and if possible, each year, this is the best way to become decisive about your goals.

You need to figure out the goals that matter most to you; this should be your life ambitions and long-term goals. Make a list of those priorities you deem important and create an action plan that will help you to achieve your life goals.

Let Go

It is crucial to consciously let go of all negative thinking and emotions that can weigh you down. Negative emotions can make you have an anxiety disorder and can lead tochronic stress.

One way to let go is by talking to a support system about how you feel about your goals, which can help you to reason clearly and give you another perspective.

Become aware of your thoughts, monitor those thoughts regularly, and be ready to get rid of those thoughts that do not serve you.

7.2. Programs that can help you to declutter your mind

7.2.1. Cognitive Behavioural Therapy

This program focuses on exploring the relationships around your feelings, behaviors, and thoughts.

During Cognitive Behavioural Therapy, a therapist will carefully walk you through your mind to uncover negative thought patterns and how they may be causing harm to you by being the source of your self-destructive beliefs and behaviors.

By addressing these negative thought patterns, you and your therapist can come up with new thought patterns that are healthier and would help you to produce healthier beliefs and behaviors. For example, if you have thoughts of low esteem (I am a failure, I can't get anything done), CBT can help you replace it with (I can do this most of the time, I may not get it right at first, but I can always try again).

Often, your therapist will give you homework between sessions where you practice replacing your negative thought with thoughts that are more realistic and positive, or your therapist can ask you to record your negative thoughts in a journal.

CBT is useful in treating anxiety disorders, bipolar disorder, schizophrenia, eating disorders, depression, and stress.

7.2.2. Exposure Therapy

This type of cognitive-behavioral therapy is mostly used to treat post-traumatic stress, obsessive-compulsive disorder, and phobias. During this therapy, your therapist will work with you to identify what triggers your anxiety and will teach you techniques to avoid the triggers or avoid reacting to those triggers. This therapy helps you to confront what triggers your concerns in a safe environment.

Two methods can be used to perform exposure therapy. One presents a small amount of triggering stimulus and escalates them overtime while the other gives a considerably large amount of the triggering stimulus all at once. Both methods will help you to cope with what triggers your anxiety, stress, worry, etc.

7.2.3. Psychodynamic Psychotherapy

This program helps you to recognize negative thinking and habits that are due to past experiences and helps you to resolve them. This type of therapy makes use of free association and open-ended questions so that you can have the opportunity to discuss whatever you have on your mind. The therapist will then work with you to unconscious patterns of negative thoughts and emotions and how they may be as a result of past experiences. By bringing you to the understanding that it was your past experiences that led to your present condition, your therapist can then guide you on how to overcome unhelpful feelings and behaviors.

7.2.4. Therapy Pets

If you spend time with domestic animals, it can reduce your symptoms of depression, stress, anxiety, pain, and fatigue. Nursing homes, hospitals, and other medical facilities are known to sometimes make use of this therapy by making use of pet animals.

Research has shown that if you spend time with pets, it can reduce your level of anxiety more than a lot of popular recreational activities. They are particularly helpful for children and veterans with PTSD.

7.3. How to Develop Self-Esteem

How you feel about yourself is very important to your happiness in life. Having a high opinion of yourself, what you do, who you are and love for yourself is one important thing that people have little of in today's society.

Some benefits of developing high self-esteem include;

- Life becomes lighter and more straightforward.

- More inner stability.

- Less self-sabotage.

- You'll be a more admirable person to your close ones and colleagues at work.

- You'll be happier.

Those are the benefit of developing good self-esteem, but how do you develop this habit? Here's how;

1.Say "Stop" to your inner critic

An excellent place to start if you want to raise your self-esteem is by learning how to replace the voice of your inner critic.

Everyone has an inner critic that often spurs us to do things to gain the acceptance of others in your life and on social media. This need to gain acceptance drags your self-esteem down as you will begin to judge yourself by how others judge you.

The inner critic is that voice inside our head that says destructive thought in your mind. For example, it says words like;

- You are not worthy of this position; it's above your technical skills.

- You aren't worthy of that girl; she will leave you for another.

- You are a bad mother.

You don't have to accept the things the inner critic says to you; there are ways to minimize them and replace this thought with more positive thinking. You can change what you think about yourself.

One way to get over the inner-critic is by stopping whatever the inner critic pipes up in your mind is to create a stop-word or stop-phrase for it.

Once the inner critic brings a thought to you, shout "Stop" in your mind. Or come up with your word or phrase that can stop the train of thought. Then refocus your thoughts to more positive things.

2. Use healthier motivational habits

To reduce the inner critic's intensity, motivate yourself to raise your self-esteem, and take positive actions.

3. Take a break for self-appreciation

Self-appreciation is very fun and straightforward, and you will notice a remarkable difference if you spend just two minutes on it every day of the month. Here's how to go about it;

Slowly take a deep breath and ask yourself this question "What are the three things I like about my life?" A few examples of answers you can give yourself are;

- What I write impacts a lot of people.

- I'm a good boss at work.

- I'm very caring and thoughtful when it comes to dogs.

These talks won't just help you build your self-esteem; they will also turn negative moods into a good one.

4. Do the right thing.

You will raise and strengthen your self-esteem when you do what you think is right. It might be a small thing like going to the gym in the morning or helping your childwith theirstudies.

To make it more effective, stay consistent in the right thing you've made up your mind to do. Make sure you take action every day.

5. Handle mistakes and failures positively

It is normal to stumble and fall if you go outside of your comfort zone. It is necessary if you want to do things that matter in life. Everyone that has got to great heights in life did; you hardly hear them talk about it. So, remember that, and when you falter try to do these things;

- Be your best friend: Rather than beating yourself up and being angry about it, ask yourself this question. Who will support me in this situation? How will the person help me? Then start imagining the person advising you.

- Find the upside: one other way to be more constructive is to focus more on opportunities and optimism. Ask yourself these questions: What can I learn from this? What benefit can I derive from this situation? These will help you to change your viewpoint on failure.

7.4. How to Develop the New You

A lot of us build up images in our heads about who we are "I'm boring, I'm suffering from depression," etc. we reiterate this point to ourselves, and we convince our mind that it's the way we are. No matter the length of time that you've been repeating these ideas to yourself, in reality, it is always changing.

I do not have any doubt in my mind that anyone can change anything they want about their life, whether it is a mental image, physical appearance, or a bad habit. If you're ready to develop the new you read through the fifteen steps below;

- Have an understanding that there is nothing that can't be changed about your life, even though it looks permanent. Think of the changes that occurred in your life from a younger age until now.

- Learn that a belief is not the truth but a thought you keep thinking.

- Have an understanding that our beliefs are not the truth; they are just things we chose to accept. For example, my favoritecolor is blue, I'm shy, etc.

- Have a realization that unless you have the desire to change, the change will never happen.

- Decide to change. If your decision to change is not deep rooted, real change will elude you.

- Take gradual steps towards the change you desire. You can run towards the peak of a hill in a flash. You have to take little steps that matter every day. Once you form a habit of taking those steps in the first few weeks, the pattern sticks, and it becomes easy from there on. If what you want to change from is an addiction, gradually reduce the craving. For example, if you're going to quit smoking, gradually reduce the number of cigarettes you smoke every day.

- Experiment with things that you find easy to change at first; this is to create the belief in yourself that if you can stop doing this, you can stop doing that.

- Choose something that you always had in mind to change, so that you will appreciate the effectiveness of your new mindset.

- To make the change real, tell some people close to you, and give yourself some accountability.

- Ignore the inner critic that keeps telling you that "you can't do this."

- When you mess up, don't give up. It's normal to mess up at times.

- When you slip back into old patterns, make a considerable effort to get out of it. Don't scold yourself; notice it, laugh at it, and try again.

- Don't let the opinions and suggestions of others weigh you down; it will take some time for them to notice the change.

- See yourself as the new you. Feel free to tell others that things are no longer the same. Say to them, "I now exercise everday", "I will not smoke again" etc.

- See the old part of you as a part of you that isgone. If your mind or a friend suggests that you should go back to your old self, say, "That was the old me." If the thoughts keep coming back, distract yourself fromthem. If a friend keeps suggesting that you revert to your old lifestyle, cut everymeans of communication with them.

Conclusion

We have touched on a number oftopics that can help you declutter your mind and reinventthe new you. The topics we touched on are what successful people do to focus their minds on their goals. Practice what is written in this book and you'll find out that there is nothing you'll aim for that is outside your reach.

The secret of harnessing the power of your mind is not in doing the right things once, it is in doing them consistently.

www.ingramcontent.com/pod-product-compliance
Lightning Source LLC
Chambersburg PA
CBHW061352250726
48657CB00004B/1456